LET US TELL IT...

HOW IT WAS,
HOW IT IS,
AND HOW IT WILL BE
IN THE FUTURE

T0145802

CSM G.P. Kotzur, USA (Ret.)

TURNER PUBLISHING COMPANY

TURNER PUBLISHING COMPANY

Author: G.P. Kotzur

Turner Publishing Company Staff:
Chief Editor: Robert J. Martin

Library of Congress
Catalog Card Number 95-60323

ISBN: 978-1-68162-344-3

TABLE OF CONTENTS

ABOUT THE AUTHOR

G.P. Kotzur served in World War II, Korea, and Vietnam. He retired as a Command Sergeant Major from the U.S. Army after 33 years of service to his country. In his own words, "I am proud to be an American." He shares some brief history and personal memories in this narrative on World War II.

Last re-up for U.S. Army Dec., 1970 at reveille, Darmstadt, Germany. (L to R) BG Joseph F.H. Cutrona administrating oath to CSM G.P. Kotzur.

BIOGRAPHY

CSM (Ret) G.P. Kotzur, was born in March 1917. He enlisted in the United States Army in October 1940 when WWII was being forced upon the United States. He fought for his country and helped bring the WWII conflagration to an end.

Kotzur received the best training the Army had to offer. This training included: many hours of field duty, shooting of weapons, and participation in two of the Louisiana maneuvers. He took Airborne training with the Division in November 1942, then moved with the division to Camp McCoy, Wisconsin.

The Division soldiers at Camp McCoy were committed to rigorous sub-arctic training which culminated in a winter maneuver in Michigan where temperatures dropped as low as 40 degrees below zero. During this sub-arctic training there were no tents or stoves for warmth. This was not a place or time for softies. Kotzur liked the training because all tasks were completed using minimum time and peak efficiency.

Kotzur fought for the Allies in Normandy for 71 consecutive days (a record for his division). Since the fighting had begun, his first hot meal was June 28 and his first river bath followed in August. Here he was fighting for Brest, France.

The efforts of Kotzur during WWII included the Battle of the Bulge. During the Big Fight, 16-19 December, there was no rest or sleep for the soldiers. The ground was covered with snow, red stained by the blood of American soldiers and blackened by the exploding gun shells. He also fought in Leipzig, another German stronghold. The German 88's had a pretty good bite to them. Positioned in Leipzig were hundreds of German Ack-Ack weapons, so the allied pilots nicknamed the area Ack-Ack Alley.

On May 7th Kotzur's division ended up in Pelsin, Czechoslovakia. Then on May 8th the Unconditional Surrender of the Axis forces was signed at Reims, Germany. Europe, America and all its Armed Forces rejoiced.

Kotzur's division had set a record for the most number of days on line in Normandy and on the Siegried Line. For many of the soldiers in his division there were 320 consecutive days of combat, with not one second spent under a roof. Kotzur was one that had to rough it, and he is proud to be listed among those soldiers.

In July, 1945, Kotzur returned to the United States. Although many of his friends told him he was crazy for doing so, he re-enlisted in the U.S. Army. His mission after the war was to enjoy hot food, hot showers, a cot, and possibly catching a wife. As it turned out, he was able to complete his mission in all categories.

Kotzur was in Japan, assigned to the 25th Infantry Division, when the Korean War broke out. This division was the second to arrive in South Korea to repel the North Korean Army. After arrival in South Korea, Kotzur's division was ordered to remain and hold Pusan until help arrived. These division soldiers had 65 days of fierce battles to contend with before their help came. It was so rough in Pusan that even the military chaplains found it safer to have a pistol on their hip rather than a prayer on their lip.

Kotzur's division was already in North Korea when the Chinese entered the war. Here the temperatures dropped as low as 75 degrees below zero. Mess sergeants warmed the troops with coffee that was "pure as an angel, strong as love, black as the devil, and hot as hell".

As the fighting in Korea wore on, the war became like a poker game; win some today and lose it back to the opponents on the next. The win/lose situation put an end to the thought of the soldiers going home by Christmas. Instead, a rotation policy was established for the troops. In August, 1951, Kotzur finally left Korea and returned to the United States.

Kotzur arrived in Vietnam in 1965 only to find more young American soldiers giving their lives for nothing. In 1966 he returned to the United States from Vietnam; it was the last war he would fight in for the United States.

Kotzur served with 9 U.S. Army divisions during his military service. His assignments have included an artillery group, a missile command, an armored calvary regiment, and (3 1/2 years) basic training centers. He has also been an advisor to the U.S. National Guard, as well as Advisor to a Foreign Army.

Kotzur marched with the United States Army for 33 years, 2 months, and 15 days. Over 30 years of his career was spent directly with his troops. He had 34 total assignments and served as First Sergeant under 22 Commanders and as Sergeant Major under 20 commanders. He took his last re-enlistment oath (administered by a general officer) at 0600 hours by the flagpole in Germany.

Effective January 1, 1974, at the age of 57, Kotzur retired ("with no regrets") from the United States Army. To him the garrison duty had been a vacation and he looked upon combat duty as the "rough" spots in his military life. In either situation, he had seen it through.

Throughout his military career Kotzur fought in three wars, earning 13 battle stars and 22 awards and decorations, including decorations for bravery in combat. He compiled over 35 months of combat duty. His name has appeared in four books, the American Stars and Stripes and in several American newspapers reflecting on his actions in combat. He has received numerous Certificates of Appreciation and Commendation for his efforts.

Since his retirement from military service Kotzur continues to serve his country. He has written many articles and materials in defense of America and her people, the United States Military Forces, and the U.S. Flag. He displays the American Flag everyday and spends his idle time with his wife, Irene. He remains close to home, because a field and combat soldier comes home to rest. He is thoroughly enjoying his golden years.

NOTE FROM THE AUTHOR

The following is written as the personal comments and opinions of myself and is not to be misconstrued as pointing a critical finger or to show a lack of respect or to decry the elected officials in any way. Instead, these comments and opinions are written with a sincere desire to point out what it took to get America started, the ups and downs of our nation and its people, the wars America has participated in, where we are now, and what must be done to get America on the right track again.

I am most grateful to Mrs. Kathy L. Mullins for her assistance in preparation of my manuscript. Kathy: a job well done!

Sincerely,

Ⓖ7ℙℛ

G.P. Kotzur

INTRODUCTION

The first Pilgrims landed in America on 21 November in 1620. These Pilgrims and those who followed shortly thereafter had to face many hardships and challenges in all aspects of their daily lives. They laid the foundation for America with the few things they brought with them to the New World. Those who could not cope with the trying tasks returned to their homelands. This New World was no place for softies or those who wanted something without working for it. There were no handouts then. There were no places for howlers to cry "Come and take care of me. I am hungry, wet and cold, and I am not healthy." Free rides were nowhere to be found. No one had a college or higher education, briefcases, or fancy clothes to wear. If they had, many of their axes would still be leaning against the trees on the east coast today. That kind of hard work the Pilgrims did calls for hard heads and strong bodies.

As the nation grew many left the east coast and headed for California in search of gold. It took the pioneers 138 days by wagon to make the long, treacherous journey. These pioneers had to fend for themselves along the way. Not all of them made it to California and had to be buried en route. Those who withstood the challenge made it to the west coast ready to start their new life in California digging for gold. They had courage and determination and knew how to use them.

The pioneers had no government inspectors telling them what they could or couldn't do. The pioneers decided if the water was safe to drink. There was no government inspection to determine if the food was fit for consumption. The pioneers decided where to build their cabins and where to send their children to school. It was the pioneer's choice whether or not to use a weapon against a thief. There were no licenses for wagons or the occasional dog. Animal droppings too close to a cabin where flies pestered sleeping babies were at the discretion of the pioneer that owned the cabin. There was no government complaining about the pollution hampering desired progress. The pioneers had a free hand to get the job done and they did it. A vast government can be an enemy to smooth and efficient progress. Just look at America now. Enough said.

The pioneers who settled this nation worked from daylight until dark, Monday through Saturday. Because their bodies craved rest, Sunday was set aside for relaxation and for those who wished to worship in the church. They had to keep pretty close to home because there was a constant need for care of the animal stock. There was little time for recreation in those days. No care for the cows meant no milk to drink or meat to eat, without hogs there was no lard, no chickens meant no eggs, and so on. These pioneers did not roll over in bed in the morning, they rolled out of bed to face the chores each day in order to survive. Family dogs were on duty 24 hours around the clock, guarding against thieves and wild beasts.

The pioneer men did the harder work like building the cabin and erecting corrals and pens for the livestock. They prepared the land for farming, removing stones by hand. Wells for water had to be dug. In addition to these chores, the men hunted game for food and trapped smaller animals for their furs for family use and to use for sale and trade. They also had to cut a great deal of wood for the family to use. No gloves were worn because only softies used gloves back then.

Pioneers made their own rope. This was important because ropes laid on the ground around the cabin kept out the snakes and most insects. Pioneers always kept harnesses and other leather goods in functional condition, and, if time permitted, set out fishing lines to provide fish meat for the family. Fishing was not a sport in those days; it was a method of survival. Some pioneers had to build strong fortifications to keep out the Indians. It was necessary for the safety of the family.

Most pioneers had to act as their own veterinarian to keep their stock healthy. They planted the crops and gave it their best shot for a good harvest. They taught their children all they knew to provide the children with the knowledge they would need to make it on their own.

The pioneer women were made of tempered steel. They never complained that their house was merely a log cabin. They used what they had and did a fine job with it. They cooked on the open fires outside, chopped wood, made the family clothing and bedding, and washed clothes on a scrub board or smooth rock. They tended their gardens and preserved the harvest, as well as meats, to keep the family fed. While working the crops they moved their kitchens to the field, when necessary, to keep the family fed. They cared for the livestock by feeding and cleaning them. Pioneer women breast fed their babies and always displayed the utmost in love for their children and husbands.

Pioneer women had to be very versatile. They were nurses when a family member was sick. They made their own butter and bread. Most of them made their own soap. And not one of them was afraid to use a gun if the husband was away. Many pioneer women knew how to make their own medicines from the natural resources the land had to offer. Pioneer women were not concerned with looking pretty. Instead, they wanted to look like hard working women who gave all their tasks 100 percent.

Vacations were unheard of in the pioneer days. Even as late as 1932, only about 13% of the women who lived in the country took an annual vacation. Most of the "country" women went to town only twice a year to buy supplies.

Pioneer women reared their children in a proper way. They taught them to be kind, not to lie and steal, and how to stand up for themselves when they were right. The children were taught not to fake anything and to do their very best in all tasks assigned to them. They were shown how to seek responsibility and to always obey the law. Pioneer women trained their daughters to be ladies and how to be good mothers.

The pioneers, both men and women, are the ones who gave America the foundation to get to where we were, at one time, the best nation in the world. America was slowly growing. People did not have much, but what they had was hard earned by them.

Eventually time passed and then came WWI. After the war ended America bounced back and things were going pretty well for most of the nation. The "Roaring Twenties" were ushered in and this gave the nation a big shot in the arm. Just as quickly as prosperity seemed to appear, the Roaring Twenties were gone. The Great Depression hit in 1929 and almost brought the United States and the rest of the world to a stand still.

THE DEPRESSION, 1929 - 1941

Even though times were hard after the depression hit in 1929, automobile production in America was on the increase. The Model A Ford was the "honey", as were a few other new cars. Just like today, each new make was better than the model before. Progress was being made in other areas, too. In the 1930's, the tractor began replacing animal farming on a wide scale. City folks wanted a car to drive and farmers wanted both. Trucks began replacing wagons and the horse-drawn buggy was fast becoming a has-been.

Electronic milking machines were being used instead of milking by hand.

As a whole, the going was much rougher for most Americans. It was a good thing that about 85% of Americans lived in farming communities then. Had all the people lived in the cities many more Americans would have starved for lack of food. Most farming communities were lucky enough to be able to grow much of the foodstuff needed to survive. Those Americans living in the cities and the poor farming areas suffered the most.

Flour, beans, and milk were the staples of the day that kept the people alive. Beans would stick to your ribs and flour gravy was usually on the table for all three meals in most homes. Milk was used various ways to provide a little more solid food. Goat milk was not uncommon in those days.

I remember the Great Depression. In those days there were times when you wished you could eat the grunt of a pig. Our livestock received special care, for they were our life's blood. Wild game, such as rabbit, was also craved. People fished, not for sport, but simply to have meat to eat. Many Americans headed out west with hopes for a better life, and some found it.

During the Depression many fathers ran out on their families. This was a doubly hard hit for the mothers and children. Some of the fathers were never heard from again. Some men committed suicide because they lost everything they had ever worked for.

People didn't have fancy clothes to wear in the depression years. Many went barefooted. Men had a hard time keeping trousers on and turned to wearing overalls. Most women made their clothes from flour sacks, including their undergarments.

Dryland farming was a hit and miss venture. Families were usually large then and there were years when the cotton crop was only 4 or 5 bales. A 500 pound bale of cotton sold for $5 per bale. Many other crops suffered due to lack of rain. When there was enough luck to pull a good corn crop, corn on the cob was enjoyed by many. There weren't very many overweight Americans seen living in the country then.

Strong courage and high spirit pulled America through the Depression years. People whistled, sang and hummed, and joked in hopes that better days would soon return. Most people were so poor that their own shadow was ashamed. One good meal a day with enough drinking water was all that was wanted. The people of these times made it on plain guts.

I remember on hot days we would add 1 tablespoon salt to every 3 gallons of drinking water to keep us from going down from heatstroke. There were many of us out in the fields. The only shade we had was when an eagle or buzzard flew over our head. There was no air conditioning then. And when we returned from the fields, we still had our daily house chores to do, like tending the stock. Everyone in the family had his duty assignments and back talk was never allowed.

In those days meat and coffee grinders received full play. The smokehouse was a very important possession and was constantly guarded against thieves. Sometimes the weather was dry, causing a water shortage. During these times the water would be hauled in at night.

On top of all the hardships brought on by the Depression, the midwest became a "Dust Bowl". Those days called for every ounce of courage if people were to make it. Humor was the one life saver that kept many going against big odds.

In the early 1940's when WWII broke out that same stock of people were just as courageous and ready to fight in the big war. When Hitler ordered his armies to invade Poland in September of 1939 the big boys in Washington were etching a plan to get into the war and still make the U.S. look like a peace loving nation. Japan solved the problem when, on 7 December 1941, they attacked American troops at Pearl Harbor. The saying goes: Old rich men start the war and young poor men die in it. War is big business and the big businessmen loaded up pretty heavy in the big war.

MOVIES

Movies with sound were introduced in the 1930"s. Even in the 1930's the movie stars were neatly dressed and looked like movie stars all the way. Dirty language was not heard neither on the screen nor on the stage. They were good movies and were made on a small fee paid to the stars. They are still being shown today and still stand out in the crowd.

Movies nowadays are not as great as the people in Washington would have us believe. Filth and dirty language have replaced neatness and professional acting.

In the 1930's and through the years following WWII the movies were pretty much clean. The cost was much lower, too. I remember in the 1930's when 10 cents would get us in to see a good clean movie. Some of these movies are still being shown on TV today. The movies back then were for everybody to see without any restrictions. It should be like that now. Why not?

MUSIC

In the old days right after the turn of the century people would often dance to simple humming and whistling. Later the harmonica and the accordion got plenty of blowing and pulling. The fiddle and guitar music were number one in the country, with the fiddle receiving most of the attention. In the cities the music of the horn was considered in better taste. The organ, if available, received much pumping. The piano was pretty much collecting dust in those days.

It was a time of popularity for religious songs because people wanted to feel that they were on God's team. Even the women sang and hummed and whistled then. Singing and whistling on the job was commonplace. Good whistlers often appeared in movies.

I still recall the dance halls out in the country. Fathers would dance with daughters and mothers would dance with their sons. Graceful dancing was the only kind of dancing allowed. Those who got too fresh on the dance floor were booted out of the dance hall.

But wars change things for the future of all. After WWI the so-called roaring 20's came about. It replaced the common style of dance with a much less graceful style that including kicks and a great deal of mobility. The Charleston and "big band" music became very popular then.

In the 1930's the music changed again. The "big band" sound went more toward swing and jazz. Dancing the "jitterbug" replaced most other forms of dance. Not all dancers were able to dance the jitterbug, but many were very good at it. Women tend to look better on the dance floor and it was even more evident when they danced the jitterbug. Honky tonks and other hot spots got most of the jitterbugging crowd.

Songs and music do not last long without changes. The number one tune or song nowadays only lasts a few days or weeks. Many men write songs about dying of a broken heart. If this were true, all men in America would be dead. As for the songs about women, there would be more women standing on their heads than on their feet if the women took the songs seriously.

In the 1930's Bob Wills and His Texas Playboys put stringed instrument music on the dance floor in America. Bob added horns, piano, and drums to give the music a spark. By adding the "beat" it made the music very danceable. Bob Wills and His Texas Playboys changed the "country" music in this country. Country music is extremely big business now.

Jimmie Rodgers and Bob Wills gave country music its foundation in America. Don't get me wrong. There were and are many others since then that were better than Rodgers and Wills, but they already had something to build on.

The "big band" and Bob Wills music have not been replaced to date. They were one of a kind. Their music was good and their musicians dressed first class or they didn't play in the band. Just as simple as that. Always the musicians had to be professional and polite or they got the boot out of the band.

WWII

WASHINGTON

President Franklin D. Roosevelt, as Commander in Chief of the Armed Forces (and half a dozen good men), functioned and operated the entire war effort from Washington. The military top leaders ran the planning, training, and the fighting to win WWII. They used very efficient policies and procedures. Outside meddling was not allowed. The Congress and Senate had to be left out if the war was to be won.

Adolph Hitler paid big money to some half-assed Americans to make noise about America staying out of the war. He knew very well that once the United States entered the war his wicked and glory days would soon be over; and they were.

MAN IS WAR

I am grateful to God, my country, the United States Army, and to the 2nd Infantry Division for having the opportunity to fight for freedom in WWII. Let us all be grateful (thankful) to all the wonderful American mothers who provided the brave sons for the military service that won WWII, allowing America to continue to enjoy her freedom and her way of life. The real heroes of WWII never made it home. A special prayer for them is always appropriate.

MILITARY DOCTORS AND NURSES

The doctors and nurses of the armed service had a big, bloody job to do. One could never express adequate thanks and appreciation for the excellent job performed by these medical professionals. The military nurses are women of tempered steel. Bloody tasks and long hours never stop them. Those who have departed. . .God rest their soul.

MILITARY WOMEN WHO BECAME PREGNANT

Pregnant female support in the Armed Services were discharged for the good of the service. Allowing pregnant females to remain in the service would have given the impression the Armed Forces were operating from the last roundup. Furthermore, the military uniform was not designed to accommodate a pregnancy. Gone are the days when officers or non-commissioned officers were heard barking out a command. "Suck in your gut, soldier! You're in the Army now." Nowadays the heavy, pregnant women could not comply with such a command.

LANGUAGE

Only the English language was permitted in the military ranks during the WWII era. All members of the military served and fought for the same cause, the United States of America.

THE PEOPLE

The United States of America, its people and its Armed Forces displayed a lot of spirit and soul during the big war. Americans put their shoulder to the wheel like a nation should. It was good to be an American in that war because many of the other countries had it plenty rough.

THE FIGHTING OF THE WAR

The fighting men in the Pacific fought a much harder war than those of us in the European Theater of Operations. They fought a wicked enemy, many tropical diseases, lack of personnel replacement, and a shortage of supplies. After the Pearl Harbor attack, the Japanese Armed Forces captured more territory in three days than did Hitler's Armed Forces in two years in Europe.

THE MILITARY WIVES IN WWII

Military wives did not whine or yearn for their daddy. Instead, they asked questions to learn if their husbands were keeping up with the single troops. They did not want to be a burden on the military or the American working class. They were not seen at the military medical centers to show their bodies around like it is seen today. They would have frowned if their men had been allowed to come home for lunch. They would have viewed this as an excuse for the men to get a noon hour quickie. They were a tough stock.

TRAINING

There were many different types of training taking place in the military during WWII. For example, some Army divisions and the U.S. Navy spent much time practicing aquatic landings. A military study showed that there would need to be about 80 aquatic landings to win the war. There were over 80 of these landings made in WWII. The three Louisiana maneuvers were good ones and provided the needed training to make the wartime land war success.

The armored units trained in the California desert. The Armor and Airborne units were new (in their infancy) and had to undergo much training to remove the rough spots before they were combat ready.

The Army also decided to organize a mountain division. This took a lot of hard work and even harder training to get the division combat ready. The Mountain Division saw combat in Italy.

The 2nd Infantry Division was moved from Fort Sam Houston, Texas, to Camp McCoy, Wisconsin and then to Michigan for cold weather training. Temperatures in Michigan fell as low as 40 degrees below zero. There were no tents or stoves. That did not stop us. It also provided good training for the soldiers' back sides. To ease mother nature in 40 below temperatures taught the soldiers the value of the element of time in cold weather.

The training in the divisions for combat was much harder. It had to be harder than combat itself if the soldiers were to find some relaxation on the battlefield. The divisions had to have it right to win the big war on the ground, and they did. The soldiers eagerly absorbed the training because they were young and had a huge job ahead of them to whip the Germans and Japanese, returning peace to the world.

OFFICER CANDIDATE SCHOOL
There were several schools of officer candidates that turned

out many good officers from the enlisted ranks. Most of them knew the men and equipment real well. They were not afraid to get with it stateside or in combat. They were a good stock of men for sure. Their level of formal education was not high, but they knew how to train and lead their soldiers. The OCS schools were a busy place.

THE WARRANT OFFICER PROGRAM

There were many good Warrant Officers in personnel, maintenance, and other assignments. They were a big help to the officer corps in that field. The Warrant Officers are still around today doing a superb job in various fields. Often they are the Commander's "butt savers."

WEST POINT

The Military Academy at West Point reduced the four year requirement to three during the war to make young officers available for combat duty. Most of these young officers were chopping at the bit. The West Point men were always ready to answer the call to duty, be it safe or dangerous. The three-year graduates welcomed the challenge.

STATESIDE

Proper training of an Army division for combat is very much like tuning a fiddle. The fiddle is not finely tuned unless all four strings on the fiddle are in tune with each other. All soldiers in the divisions were trained to fight on a division level after they had completed their training on the unit level. They were all finely tuned to the other. The Division Commander was the fiddler. The Division Artillery Commander played the upright bass to add the heavy artillery beat to the firing on the training ranges and in combat.

On the orders of the commanders no one screwed with the soldiers assigned to rifle companies, the machine gun crews, the anti-tank companies, the mortar platoons, tank companies, the combat engineers, or the artillery soldiers assigned to firing batteries. They are the ones who win the war on the ground. They make commanders from top to bottom look good and make them heroes. They were number one with the Generals.

The commanders and their officers were held responsible for the training and everything the enlisted men did or failed to do.

Free rides were not allowed. The staff officers and the sergeant majors were not permitted to meddle in the Commander's and First Sergeant's business. Only a few tried, and those who did ended up with a black eye or bloody nose, or both. It was a sound and efficient policy. That is the way it had to be if the divisions were to be good ones, stateside and on the battlefield.

The soldiers were always on sure footing because the sense of urgency was enforced to the fullest extent at all times. The War Department (now the Department of Defense) also knew the status of the training and combat readiness of the United States Army. The entire army marched in step then, with 100% adherence to training schedules.

It was the responsibility and duty of the officers and non-commissioned officers to whip the divisions and their soldiers into combat readiness and, therefore, capable of victory on the battlefield. Officer and non-commissioned officer (short) classes were conducted in the evenings or in the afternoons to remove the rough spots from training and elsewhere in operations. Field problems that got off on the wrong foot were halted immediately. Corrections were made and the field problems resumed.

There were only a few schools on post. Soldiers were not trained for combat in military schools. They were trained in the units and divisions to assure a victory on the battlefield. Furthermore, the officers and non-commissioned officers would have frowned on such practices. They would have made it known, loud and clear, that training the soldiers for combat was their responsibility. It was an honor, as well as being fun, to be an officer or non-commissioned officer in the WWII era.

Let's not forget that Army divisions are like ball clubs and some are better than others. The officers and the non-commissioned officers in the division are what made the difference.

The Division Commanders trained their own staff in all aspects of operations. They thoroughly knew the duties of the Regimental Commanders and their staffs. The Division Artillery Commander also trained his staff. In the 2nd Infantry Division, DIVARTY Commander picked the S-3 operations officers for the battalion under his command. In the artillery units the S-3 and S-4 are the most important officers in the battalion. They have to be good or the battalion will bring up the rear in the division.

Before WWII broke out, the Company and Battery Commanders were First Lieutenants. The Battalion Commanders were Majors and Regimental Commanders were Lieutenant Colonels. It was not unusual to see a Brigadier General commanding a division. Officers who didn't cut it in the officer ranks were converted to enlisted status and assigned to troop duty.

The Sergeant Major rank was E-7. Those promoted to the rank of Sergeant Major were usually from infantry rifle companies or artillery firing batteries. The Army could not afford to have chair warmers for Sergeant Majors.

Division Commanders lead their troops on the foot marches, always ahead of the troops to show their guts and set an example. All other commanders did the same. They were true commanders in those days.

There is no way our military forces would have been able to whip the enemy in 3 years, 8 months, and 25 days if commanders in WWII had to depend on the centralized promotion system currently in use. Back then commanders knew the men and promoted their personnel to achieve the most efficient team to get the job done. They didn't have to pay any attention to a GT score on Form 20. They wanted and needed good trainers and leaders. The enlisted men got a fair shake in the promotion system then, with no time or place for palm greasers and brown nosers. The officer promotion system was much better then, too. Polar complexioned and tenderfoot soldiers had very little chance of advancing. Promotion was an honor bestowed on the most deserving.

MOVEMENT OF THE UNITED STATES ARMY OVERSEAS

When it came to moving the U.S. Army overseas the the Navy came through like a champ. This was made possible by the fact that the U.S. Government was standing on both legs.

Instead of borrowing ships, the United States was selling and leasing ships to foreign nations. Yes, that was the United States back then. The Americans could be heard to say how America was clicking in all aspects.

The Congress and the Senate were not allowed to meddle in military affairs and the production of war materials. Things were in place because they had to be and America had only one President.

Again, it was very fruitful for Germany and Japan to instigate WWII and then lose the war to the Allied forces. The American taxpayers have been forced to fund the costly operations which ensued after the war. They have paid out billions in support of those countries, with nothing to show for it in return. This has caused the U.S. military leaders to put foreign nations above the security of the United States. This has been a major effort on their part because, with the aimless people in Washington, they have to rob Peter to pay Paul to make ends meet.

The American taxpayers are not funding a military force to guard America. Instead, they are funding military puppets at the beck and call of foreign nations. This fact is difficult for the U.S. military personnel to cope with because of family life disruptions. Children of military personnel take the brunt of the hardship because of the many changes in schools and family life. The people in Washington responsible for these policies cannot identify with the hardship caused by these policies because they never had to cope with a lifestyle like that of military personnel.

If the current policies regarding troops overseas are to be maintained, overseas governments should be made to pay 85% of the cost to finance our presence there. There should be no more free rides. The officials in Washington appear to be afraid that the foreign nations might not like the United Stated if we discontinue our "babysitting" service and require them to do their own work. I say let them get mad at us. It just might be a change for the better. It's time for Americans to heat up and get mad. It's not against the law for Americans to get angry (yet).

WORLD WAR II IN AMERICA: A NATION IN ACTION

A PROUD AMERICAN REMEMBERS

August 14th, 1945, 50 years ago. Certainly we need to pause a moment and look back; we need to look back to remember, to feel the emotions of pride and sorrow. Perhaps you will smile a little, or perhaps you will cry some. Most important of all, take the time to remember.

There are many of you who can't remember, for it's too long ago. But even you can take a moment to feel just a little of what your parents and friends and relatives lived through - or didn't live through.

Surely the 50th Anniversary of the end of WWII is an occasion to pause. . . and reflect. A time to remember when America was a nation in action.

THE TROOPS

September 1, 1939 - Germany invades Poland. The United States forces numbered only 335,000 men at this time and their equipment was badly outdated.

December 7, 1941 - Japan attacks Pearl Harbor. By then the United States Armed Forces had grown to 1,800,000 men. This was really a small force, but the officers and noncommissioned officers knew their jobs, the equipment, and their men. They were well disciplined and were proud of the United States Military and its uniform. They displayed the utmost respect for country and flag. They sought responsibility and craved duty. Military life was their only business.

By 1945 the number of men and women in uniform serving their country reached 16,112,000. The women numbered 320,000. Women were not permitted to serve in combat units, but did an outstanding job in the assignments they were permitted to hold. No women were permitted in the male troop areas, including the wives of the married troops. There just wasn't any time for the "best squeeze".

Just where did all our troops come from? Volunteers accounted for 38.8% of our service men and women, while 61.2% were draftees. The Secretary of War (now the Secretary of Defense) drew the first number of the draft - number 158. Of the 17,955,000 men examined for induction, 35.8% were rejected as physically or mentally unfit for military service.

The average duration of military service then was 33 months. Of our total service members, 73% went overseas, spending an average of 16.2 months abroad. Some of the enlisted personnel (38.8%) had rear echelon assignments: administrative, technical, support, or manual labor jobs. The average base pay for enlisted personnel was $71.33 per month, while officers averaged $203.50 per month. Nurses, totaling 60,000, were recruited for military service, with 32,500 of them serving overseas.

There were over 80 divisions formed for the WWII effort, including a huge Navy and Army Air Corps. The European Theater of Operations claimed 62% of the war effort because it was decided that Germany must be eliminated from the war first. The

Bavarian Bad Wolf (Hitler) was to be de-fanged; his weapons and marching hobnail boots silenced.

There are three vital "M's" in warfare: Men, Money, and Munitions. War and national defense became the world's largest business. Sound military leadership with discipline, positive training programs, ample supplies and modern operable weapons won WWII. The Armed Forces were organized on firepower. According to one soldier, "We gave the enemy hell and whipped them."

AT HOME
"We Make the War Goods So Our Boys Can Give Them Hell and That They Did"

Americans rose to their feet after the Japanese attack on Pearl Harbor and let the enemy and the world know that this was the United States of America. The first major step that had to be taken was organizing American industries. By 1945 200,000 companies were in full swing, turning out military hardware not only for the United States, but for other countries as well. By the end of the war the lend-lease account showed that the United States has supplied foodstuff and war materials valued at approximately $50 billion.

Individual Americans were doing more. Much more. They purchased $200 billion worth of War Bonds. Movie theaters (numbering 12,000) in the United States were showing newsreels on the war; clippings that encouraged the American people because they could see how well their men were doing. Hollywood did a good job of promoting the sale of War Bonds by producing war motion pictures, and with the Hollywood Canteen for the Armed Forces Personnel. The war encompassed everything the American people did - no lives went untouched, not even for one day. Even at the movies! Farmers, totalling 6 million, joined the war effort by producing enough farm products on the home front to meet the U.S. needs and the needs of a hungry world.

Meanwhile the Red Cross and its volunteers were hard at work. Wars are a bloody business. During WWII there were 291,557 Americans killed in action and 670,846 wounded. The American Red Cross had 10,000,000 blood donor volunteers - the largest in medical history. It took tons, not gallons, to keep the blood banks going with $2 billion expended in funds. The Red Cross ladies did an excellent job serving troops all over the world. The American Red Cross and the military chaplains handled the emergencies and the personal problems of the troops.

The mothers, wives and sweethearts at home did so much. The greatest morale booster for all the troops were letters from home. Food went untouched if there was a letter from home. Also, there were all kinds of patriotic songs then. The most impressive were: "God Bless America", "There is a Spangled Banner Waving Somewhere", and "Smoke on the Water". All were morale boosters.

The trains and busses played a very important part in the war effort, transporting troops within the country and to ports for departure to overseas. Many men kissed their wives or sweethearts for the last time at the train and bus stations.

MAXIMUM SIMPLICITY EQUALS MAXIMUM EFFICIENCY

This writer served with the Second Infantry Division, known as the "Second to None Division". This division was selected by the War Department as a test division for the entire army. The results were forwarded to Washington as a guide to follow for implementation in other divisions.

It was a simple theory. Maximum simplicity was practiced to the fullest extent, with minimum repeats. Maximum participation by all personnel was demanded and all troops took part in combat training. Morale was high because military morale stems from efficient training and well organized combat units and, most importantly, when the fighting forces are permitted to secure victory on the battlefield. There wasn't such a thing as a good garrison soldier then. All men in the military were trained to fight, and most of them got a good taste of it.

The Armed Forces was a well put together team. They could be seen on the streets in a town, as many as 25,000 strong, then four hours later they would be gone. The military could move, shoot, and communicate. They did their field training with radio silence.

There were only a few telephones in Headquarters buildings. This produced good planning, with no charts on walls or fancy furniture and rugs in offices. Often clipboards served as a desk for the Lieutenants. Paperwork was almost zero. There were no personal coffee pots.

The clubs and cafeterias on post were closed until after retreat.

The men ate in the mess halls and did everything as a team. The "tales" one heard from officers and sergeants in the bars were never committed in combat.

There wasn't much attention paid to the waistline. Organizing big fighting forces is pretty much like organizing a big party. Half pints and pints are fine for a small party, but to have a really good one, fifths, quarts, and half gallons must be included. The heavy men in the military certainly made good mess stewards, maintenance people, administrative, finance, and medical personnel. Further, men lose weight in battle when the going gets rough. The pint size become corks. In those days efficiency was preferred over a trim waistline.

GOOD, HARD TRAINING PRODUCED GOOD, BRAVE MEN

Wars are fought with young men in the combat units: officers, O-2 through O-5, and enlisted men E-2 through E-6. Promotions during WWII went to those who were best suited to train and to lead their men; those capable of securing a victory on the battlefield. Personnel were assigned to fit the fighting team. "Palm greasing" and "brown nosing" had no place here and was not allowed.

It took a lot of hard and fast work to train the over 16 million military personnel. Training fields, camps, posts, and schools, numbering 1,200, were required to train the troops. Many had to be quartered in tents and never did get to sleep in barracks before they were shipped overseas to fight the war. A personal memory was basic training during October and November with no hot water available!

Shortly after the attack on Pearl Harbor the military mission, training and all other aspects of military duty and operations, became a serious business. America was trading space for time. All operations were like a tight ball game riding on every pitch. Promptness was enforced to the fullest extent, with the element of time being money. Duty was placed above all else. Lesson plans came from a 3x5 card. Hard training, long hours, the enemy, and harsh weather did not stop them. They were the best Armed Forces that ever marched on God's earth. They fought a war on land, sea, and sky (worldwide) and won.

The American people were proud of their men. These men were brave and had the guts to fight a war and win. A total of 434 Medals of Honor were awarded. They all aimed straight. These men were easy to train because they knew how to work hard. Military equipment always came first because a soldier with operable equipment in his hands lives longer on the battlefield. Non-operational equipment gets men killed in war.

Physical training and the long road marches separated the sheep form the goats. The forced foot marches tested one to ascertain if he had 100% to offer. The water canteen with water in it was the soldier's best friend The men will never forget the foot blisters incurred on those marches.

Troops were kept informed in ranks where possible. A soldier's mind feeds on the information that pertains to his functions and operations. A well-informed military force is a better, stronger one. Those who did not keep their men properly informed were temporary commanders or temporary sergeants. The reason this procedure worked so well is because the military was organized: officers, then non-commissioned officers, the men below the non-commissioned officers, and lastly, the prisoners.

The personnel wore the military uniform and rendered the hand salute with a high sense of pride. Their respect for the country and flag was unquestionable. They proudly stood reveilles and retreats. If anyone said anything bad (to them) about America they ended up with a bloody nose.

SICK CALL

Sick call was held in the barracks by the enlisted medic assigned to the unit. He sorted them out and was a tough soldier, not one to give in to ear bending or faking.

The officer doctors were twice tougher than the enlisted men. There was much tonsillitis among the men then. Only few had their tonsils removed. My own rotted out while marching and fighting the war.

The soldiers could not fool the doctor in combat, either. Our battalion doctor grew up in the country and well knew the strength of the aspirin. Constipation, at least the faked type, was ignored by the good doc. Only a big case of pneumonia would get the soldiers to the hospital for a very short stay.

THE NORMANDY INVASION

Plenty of fast and hard work had to be done in America before the Normandy Invasion. American industries numbering 200,000 went into action around the clock, turning out war goods and military hardware of all types. Over 60 million Americans took their places on the production lines.

To weaken the German forces, their troops had to be defeated in north Africa, Tunisia, Sicily, Italy, Anizo, and elsewhere abroad. The U.S. and British Air Forces had to destroy the gas and oil production and their storage areas. Other targets included war munitions factories, railroads, bridges and main highways. These huge losses had to be replenished, both personnel and hardware, and was very costly to the Germans. Because it was decided that Germany must be taken out of the war first, the fighting forces in the Pacific were compelled to fight that wicked enemy on only 34% of United States war effort.

American troops in Europe were stationed in many places. Many had to undergo additional training to be ready for the big fight in Europe. Many hours were spent on aquatic landing training. Waterproofing equipment also received full attention and it was done until it was done right.

The Supreme Allied Headquarters spent many months in preparation for the operation of the Overlord Plans. The plan had to be exact. There was no room for error.

The Berlin news woman by the name of Berlin Sally put on a full payload of propaganda on her radio show in hopes of discouraging the allied troops. We paid no attention to her hen cackling.

In early June the troops were loaded on ships in a top secret effort. Blackouts were enforced to the fullest extent. Once things were just right, General Dwight Eisenhower gave the go ahead. The weather forecasts were studied closely before and on 6 June. Although the weather was not completely satisfactory on 6 June, the decision was made to strike the Normandy beaches anyway. There were five beaches: Utah, Omaha, Gold, Juno, and Sword. The U.S. Army strike divisions landed on Utah and Omaha beaches. That night there were German air attacks on the beach area. The skies were lit up with hundreds of anti-aircraft gunfire. The Germans did not return for another try.

The Germans had Omaha Beach more strongly defended than the other four beaches. They also had the 352nd Infantry Division to reinforce their forces at Omaha. It was a rough spot, but the can and will do American attitude and their high spirits got the job done.

The American Ranger Battalion had it plenty rough in that operation. None of the strike forces found it easy on that day. The 2nd Infantry Division landed on Omaha Beach, D-Day plus one. The division went on line between the 1st and 29th Divisions. The 2nd Infantry Division Artillery Howitzers were firing from 2,000 to 10,000 yards. For all the U.S. and Allied troops every inch of ground and every shot counted.

On 6 June there were a large number of small boats zipping through the water. Explosions could be seen and heard, evidence of the combat engineers destroying land mines and beach obstacles. We saw German gun shells hitting the beach and water near us. The military ambulance vehicles could be seen bumper to bumper carrying the dead and wounded.

The going was slow for the Allied troops. The German soldiers had been given orders to die on the ground they stood, rather than retreat. For example, from 6 - 14 June some of the fighting forces had pushed inland only about 25 kilometers, encountering strong resistance all the way.

The U.S. Navy played the utmost role in the Normandy landings. The Navy had it together in that operation. Their vast firepower was shown here. The sailors went without sleep for many hours in the Normandy Invasion. For all of them "duty called".

I do not know whose side God was on in that battle, but on (about) 19 June a strong storm badly damaged the artificial port at Omaha Beach which slowed the delivery of the much needed supplies to continue the battle. An all out effort was made to capture the port of St. Lo. The Germans were driven out and the port was available for Allied use.

The OP's had to be manned in trees. The German 88's kept the OP personnel on the alert. The OP's were very important in that operation, as well as being very dangerous. The Germans were very accurate shooters. There was plenty of firing for the American artillery (Howitzers) which consisted of many rounds of ammunition, needed to break up the German attacks. The Navy artillery also did a superb job on the enemy with their artillery. In military ranks that is called good teamplay.

I can't speak for the other American divisions, but on 23 June the 2nd Infantry Division commenced firing Time On Target (TOT's), which was hell on earth for the Germans and their equipment. The captured German prisoners of war told it best of the wicked, deadly TOT's. The Americans are still grateful the Germans did not have the same capabilities to throw at us.

On 11 June an enemy plane bombed the A Battery rear echelon, setting afire an ammunition truck, two ammo trailers, and a shop truck, killing four men and wounding five. This was the first real taste of war for the men of A Battery. There were other deaths in the battalion personnel in the fight for Normandy.

Following the Trevieries and Cerisy offensive, the division held it through 10 July. During this period all arms were working on means and methods of hedgerow fighting and the tactics to be employed against Hill 192. The infantry, engineers, and tankers practiced as an assault team using demolition charges to break through thick hedgerows. A young ordnance sergeant solved that problem. He devised a blade from the spikes of a German C beach obstacle. They were attached to tanks and their sharp scoop plunged into and tore the hedgerows apart as the tanks moved forward. Commanders and tankers were a bit impressed by this.

On the morning of 11 July the assault on Hill 192 began with heavy artillery preparation fires. Troops of the 38th and 23rd Infantry, tankers and a combat engineer battalion advanced behind the Division Artillery gun shells. As a support effort, the infantry mortars did an excellent job laying down their fires on the enemy. The artillery observers fulfilled their obligation, calling for artillery fire on the enemy. Hill 192 fell into Division's hands about noon. The 12the Filed Artillery Battalion fired about 90 tons of steel in the battle for the hill. The Germans did not roll over backwards to give it up. The Hill was a strategic point, providing the Germans with good observation of the entire Normandy area.

The Division soldiers completed an enormous task here. A big victory on the battlefield is always good to soup up the troops. The next day the battalion moved forward. This was 14 July, Bastille Day. The Cerisy la Foret, which the battalion passed through, was gaily decorated with flags, bunting and signs welcoming and thanking the liberating American Army.

On 23 July the battalion got four German 10.5 cm Howitzers. Those had been captured by the infantry and turned over to the Ordnance Commander. The Division Artillery Commander jumped at the chance to use their own weapons against the Germans. The Battalion S-4 found 4,000 rounds of ammunition for the guns. American sights were mounted on them. On 25 July the guns were fired to give the Germans a taste of their own medicine. The Germans were taken aback by the fact there were many "duds" in their ammunition stock. War is full of tricks for both sides.

The battle at Normandy was a good fight. I don't know about the other divisions in the fight, but the Second to None Division had 71 days without a break since their landing on Omaha Beach on 7 June. Their first hot meal was 28 June and the first river bath was not until August.

The First United States Army and its soldiers can take a bow for doing most of the "hard" fighting in the battle of Normandy. They were instrumental in the defeat of the Germans.

General George S. Patton landed his Third Army in Normandy after the beachhead was secured. In short order, he surrounded the entire German Seventh Army. Yet, he was ordered not to close the gap between the American and British Armies. This was left up to General Bernard Montgomery. General Montgomery did bridge the gap, approximately two weeks later, but allowed many of the Germans to escape and continue to fight in other areas. Montgomery's forces were not ready in Normandy, and were never completely ready throughout the duration of WWII.

On 25 July the American and Allied forces broke out of Normandy. General Patton's Third Army was assigned the task of chasing the Germans back to German soil. This he did, shooting the Germans in the butt while en route.

Adolph Hitler actually did the Allies a big favor in the Battle of Normandy when he denied Field Marshall Erwin Rommel permission to withdraw out of the U.S. Army artillery range in order to regroup. Hitler told Rommel that German soldiers do not retreat from the battlefield. The Germans were clobbered. Hitler's orders saved many American lives in that battle.

The American news media was left out of the Battle of Normandy. Their silver tongues had to be kept silent to insure a successful undertaking in Normandy.

The victory at Normandy was very costly. But it had to be done, and it was done. See the following data on the overall operation:

THE LARGEST BATTLE IN THE HISTORY OF MANKIND

THE BATTLE

Duration	76 Days
Combatants	3,120,000
U.S. Combatants	1,842,000
Ships(war andtransport)	6,900
Allied Aircraft	11,590
Casualties (dead and wounded)	367,000
U.S. Casualties	127,000
U.S. Dead	31,000

COUNTRIES WITH TROOPS ENGAGED

United States	France
Canada	Great Britain
Holland	Norway
Germany	Poland
Belgium	Greece
Luxembourg	Czechoslovakia

AREA OF BATTLE

Battle Front	135 km
Land Area	18,249 sq. km.
Normandy Population (1944)	1,113,000
Civilian Dead	8 - 10 Thousand
Buildings Destroyed	12,420

It took a team effort from all the troops fighting in Normandy. The Signal Corps had a huge job to do to keep the many hundreds of telephone lines operational. The Combat Engineers had the dangerous job of removing and destroying enemy mines, and keeping the roads and bridges usable. The Quarter Master personnel had a very heavy workload to cope with, and then there was the bloody job for all the medical personnel. The Airborne Divisions jumped behind the enemy lines on D-Day and there were many who did not come back alive. Yes, it took team play from all the soldiers to get the enormous task of Normandy accomplished.

Let us not leave out the most battle-tested troops of that era.

They landed on the beach in southern France on 15 August, 1944. They were the ones who had already defeated the Germans in Africa, Tunisia, Italy and Anizo. These well seasoned soldiers completed another huge task when they helped liberate France and the rest of Europe.

Normandy was not the only invasion in WWII. There were over 80 of them made throughout the war. Some were small and some were not so small, but they all called for many hours of hard work and preparation prior to their execution. The Normandy Invasion was critical to bringing the war to an end in Europe and it finally did, 11 months and 2 days later.

The Germans were defeated in Normandy and there was a victory parade held in Paris. But this was still not the end of the war. Supply lines became very long and the famous Red Ball Truck Line had to be established. The Infantry Divisions, as well as many other American Divisions, had to furnish both trucks and men to get the job done. To shorten the long supply lines, Brest had to be captured to be used as a port for the Allies.

Brest was a well fortified stronghold, with 60,000 German troops. The U.S. VIII Corps, comprised of three American Divisions (the 2nd, 8th, and the 29th), took less than one month to defeat the Germans at Brest. Their orders were to hold out for at least 90 days. There was air support from the U.S. and British war planes, which proved to be very destructive to Brest and the German troops, not to mention a great help to the Allied ground troops.

After the fall of Brest, we were trucked to the area to take a look at it. After seeing the rubble of Normandy and Brest, there was no doubt in our mind that war is completely dumb and totally stupid.

After the battle at Brest ended, the division (in October) joined many other Army Divisions on the Siegfried Line. We stayed there until 10 December when the division was replaced by the 106th U.S. Division. That is where the Germans kicked off the Battle of the Bulge, 16 December 1944. They struck at the 99th Infantry Division to the 106th Infantry Division's left. Both division were somewhat green (inexperienced), and were pretty much butchered by the Germans. The 2nd Infantry Division was on line to the left of the 99th Division. We got to prove our fighting skills in that vast battle. Yes, Army Divisions are like ball clubs, and some are better than others. Enough said.

THE BATTLE OF THE BULGE

A SOLDIER'S GREATEST DAY IS WHEN HE SHOOTS;
THE AMERICAN ARTILLERY PROVED THE MOST
DISASTROUS AGAINST THE GERMAN SOLDIERS AND
THEIR ARMOR IN THAT BATTLE

In the first days of the Battle of the Bulge 81,000 American soldiers gave it their best shot and held the 50 mile front against 250,000 German soldiers (and at least 250,000 German soldiers in reserve). The ground was covered with God's white snow, stained red with American blood. There was no rest or sleep for the soldiers 16 through 19 December. They hung in there against all odds, causing the Germans to fall behind in their time table. On 19 December the German armor started to die from gasoline starvation and so did the fighting spirit of the German soldiers. The Germans desperately needed the rich gasoline and food dumps only a few miles away.

Help for the American soldiers finally arrived on 20 December. Before it was over, 29 American Divisions (plus many non-division units) were committed to the battle. The following is a listing of those divisions and their commanders:

Supreme Headquarters Allied Forces	General Dwight Eisenhower
12th U.S. Army Group	Lt. General Omar N. Bradley
First U.S. Army	Lt. General Courtney H. Hodges
V Corps	Maj. General Leonard T. Gerow
First Infantry Division	Brig. General Clift Andrus
Second Infantry Division	Maj. General Walter M. Robertson
9th Infantry Division	Maj. General Louis A. Craig
78th Infantry Division	Maj. General Edwin P. Parker
99th Infantry Division	Maj. General Walter E. Lauer
VII Corps	Maj. General Joseph L. Collins
Second Armored Division	Maj. General Ernest W. Harmon
Third Armored Division	Maj. General Maurice Rose
83rd Infantry Division	Maj. General Robert C. Macon
84th Infantry Division	Brig. General Alexander R. Bolling
XVIII Airborne Corps	Maj. General Matthew B. Ridgeway
7th Armored Division	Maj. General Robert W. Hasbrouck
30th Infantry Division	Maj. General Leland S. Hobbs
75th Infantry Division	Maj. General Fay B. Prickett

82nd Airborne Division	Maj. General James M. Gavin
106th Infantry Division	Maj. General Alan W. Jones
III Corps	Maj. General John Millikin
Third U.S. Army	Lt. General George S. Patton
4th Armored Division	Maj. General Hugh J. Gaffey
6th Armored Division	Maj. General Robert W. Grow
26th Infantry Division	Maj. General Willard S. Paul
35th Infantry Division	Maj. General Paul W. Baade
90th Infantry Division	Maj. General James A. Van Fleet
VIII Corps	Maj. General Troy H. Middleton
9th Armored Division	Maj. General John W. Leonard
11th Armored Division	Brig. General Charles S. Kilburn
17th Airborne Division	Maj. General William M. Miley
28th Infantry Division	Maj. General Norman D. Cota
47th Infantry Division	Brig. General Frank L. Cullin, Jr.
101 Airborne Division	Brig. Gen. Anthony C. McAuliffe
	Maj. General Maxwell D. Taylor
XII Corps	Maj. General Manton S. Eddy
4th Infantry Division	Maj. General Raymond O. Barton
5th Infantry Division	Maj. General S. Leroy Irwin
10th Armored Division	Maj. Gen. William H.H. Morris, Jr.
8th Infantry Division	Maj. General Horace L. McBride
U.S. Air Force in Europe	General Carl Spaatz
British Army	F.M. Sir Bernard L. Montgomery

THE BRITISH IN THE BATTLE OF THE BULGE

The Brits had few more than 200 soldiers killed in the Battle of the Bulge. Winston Churchill and British General Bernard Montgomery highly commended the American fighting men for a job well done in this big battle, while their troops sipped tea. General George S. Patton said it best about Montgomery: "The little fart".

The British made it sound like the Americans did not know what they were doing while fighting the war in Europe. The Americans had over 40 Army divisions fighting in the European Theater. Montgomery finally got to command about half of the American troops in the Bulge, like he was Mr. Know It All. It took a 2-star U.S. Army General to tell him that the United States had 40 divisions to the European's 19 divisions. These words caused Montgomery to put his beret on straight and get on with fighting the big battle. Montgomery wanted to wait like he had done in Normandy, but the American Generals did not fall for that horsestuff. When the weather cleared, the U.S. and British Air Force were put to full use and gave the Germans hell.

KEY PERSONNEL IN A MILITARY UNIT

The following is a listing and brief description of some of the key personnel of a military unit during WWII. Without competent individuals to fill these positions, any military unit would be hampered in its mission. I thought I would mention these forgotten men and the responsibility of their positions. They worked hard and earned high praise for their efforts.

THE SUPPLY SERGEANTS
For some unknown reason they never looked like a line sergeant. When the going was rough in field training and on the battlefield, the supply sergeant was the only one who looked clean by comparison. They did a good job like all the others. Those assigned to infantry units had huge turnovers in footwear, uniforms and weapons.

THE COMPANY OR BATTERY CLERK
This clerk had the Morning Report to prepare every day, he delivered the mail, took money on payday to purchase money orders for the soldiers, and usually displayed a smile regardless of time or place. The clerk usually did not look good marching. They were call the "Morale" because they handled the unit mail. They, too, always did an outstanding job. They enjoyed being able to type "morale high" on the Morning Report. They were, and still are, the First Sergeant's sidekick. They have to be men of sound patience to keep from tearing the telephone off the orderly room wall and throwing it outside. The Company or Battery Clerks were usually liked by all the men in the unit.

THE FIRST SERGEANT
He always has been, and always will be, the number one soldier in the Army. They have always been underpaid for the job they do and the responsibility they have to cope with. They make the best Sergeant Majors upon promotion to the E-9 rank.

THE OPERATION SERGEANT

The operation Sergeant is the number one on the staff at Headquarters. He is very much like a First Sergeant in the respect that he is never at a loss for something to do. His work is never done.

THE BATTALION OPERATION S-3 AND THE BATTALION S-4

These are two key officers in the battalion whether in peace or in war. All battalion operations hinge on their actions and needs. The best individuals for these jobs are the ones who have commanded a rifle company or firing battery. These positions must be held by competent hands or the battalion will bring up the rear in the division.

THE MOTOR SERGEANTS

The motor sergeants had many millions of vehicles to maintain and keep moving. During war time this was a never ending battle for the motor sergeants.

PERSONNEL SERGEANTS

With over 16 million military personnel in the ranks in the WWII era, the personnel sergeants were pretty busy. They were responsible for promotions, reductions of personnel, reassignments, awards, and a multitude of other tasks. They were also responsible for payroll then. At the end of the war discharge orders numbered up in the millions. Thousands of copies were needed for school personnel and Basic Training Centers and Navy Boot Camps.

THE MESS SERGEANTS

The Mess Sergeant's job ran 7 days a week. When assigned to an infantry unit during war, the mess sergeant often had to shoot his way through road blocks to get the chow to the hungry troops.

THE MESSENGER

Another job that required shooting your way through road blocks was the messenger. They had a rough job, but they came through.

THE 2ND INFANTRY DIVISION IN THE BULGE FIGHT

Because of a commitment elsewhere the 2nd Infantry Division did not enter the Battle of the Bulge until 17 December. The German High Command ordered the 1st SS Panzer and the 12th Panzer Divisions (the flower of the German Army) to attack the 2nd Infantry Division.

Army divisions are like ball clubs; some are better than others. The Germans ran into a rock solid wall when they attacked the soldiers of the renowned 2nd Infantry Division. The Germans quickly learned there was nowhere to go for them.

The 2nd Infantry Division soldiers became troops of tempered steel and fought bravely and with vigor. The two U.S. Army divisions to the 2nd Infantry's right were overrun by Germans and cut to pieces. The Artillery Division staff officers were adjusting artillery fires on the enemy from the windows of their headquarters building. The Division Commander committed the Headquarters personnel (the chair strength) to the battle and they engaged the enemy in hand to hand combat.

The Artillery Division firing battery soldiers fired many thousands of rounds of ammunition on the Germans, which was hell on earth to the German soldiers and their armor. All soldiers in the division were committed to doing something, such as digging trenches for the infantry soldiers to fall back into if necessary. All available trucks were busy hauling ammunition. The firing battery officers helped to shift the over 6 ton howitzers, or did other chores.

Enemy artillery shelling was heavy at times, but it did not cause the infantry soldiers to cave in or even to slow the Artillery Division howitzer firing. The Germans fired their artillery from maps, which was no match for the American artillery. The American Artillery Battalion used the Fire Direction Procedure (FDC), which was the best in the world. The 12th Field Artillery Battalion grouped the communications personnel into seven teams. Telephones were working and the artillery forward observers did a superb job of calling for artillery fires on the enemy.

The 12th Field Artillery Battalion was shooting a complete circle in all directions. From 17 through 19 December the battalion fired 3,470 rounds of ammunition. On these days alone we fired 170 tons of steel. Throughout the month of December we fired a total of 19,050 rounds of ammunition. That is a lot of steel. The artillery soldiers never go into reserve. Their job is simply to shoot.

The Infantry soldiers always take the heavy brunt of the war. I wish I knew the amount of ammunition fired in our division, but I do not. I do know that all gun barrels were hot. The Combat Engineers did an excellent job, as always. They blew out bridges, laid mines, kept roads open and functional as best they could.

The tank destroyers also did an outstanding job shooting it out with the enemy. Their losses were heavy. The Division Signal Company had much wire splicing and replacing to do in the fight. The tankers found the battle to be very much like a Western movie, using tanks instead of pistols. It was very difficult to play a cowboy with a tank.

On 20 December the two overrun U.S. Army divisions were replaced with two more U.S. Army divisions. General Patton's Third Army also arrived to the area after a long road march of approximately 100 miles. There was plenty of troop movement from several other areas as well. The wounded and those killed in action had to be replaced at once.

It's a good thing the U.S. Army had many army wheel vehicles to transport the troops and supplies. The truck drivers and the chiefs of those vehicles deserved and earned a high praise from all. Long hours and long miles did not stop them. The vehicles made for use in WWII were well manufactured and were not a junk of junks. The trucks were dependable transportation.

Nothing much has been said about the fact that the Germans spoiled the planned Christmas party for the 101st Airborne Division at Bastogne when they bombed it out on 24 December. There was no time for a Christmas party, anyway. We were there to fight and whip the Germans. When the Germans jumped their paratroopers behind us in the Bulge, we had the cooks and clerks to police them up. The Battle of the Bulge was much harder to fight than the Battle of Normandy. During the Battle of the Bulge the weather itself was an enemy. Soldiers ran double time in place to keep their feet from freezing. It was at least 4 degrees below zero and there was little use for a bath towel on the battlefield, so they were used as scarves for necks and faces. At one point it was so cold and frozen that military vehicles were not permitted on the roads. Only kitchen trucks and ambulances were allowed on the roads until further notice.

The military schools of higher learning (for officers) teach that, when in combat, a corner must be held to deny the enemy his accomplishments. Well, the 2nd Infantry Division did just that when it held Elsenborn, Belgium like a rock. The snow and ground around the towns of Krinklet and Rocherath were red with American blood and black from shell smoke. The soldiers here fought bravely and with vigor.

There were many tanks destroyed or rendered useless just on plain hard fighting and guts. Mines were laid on roads when the enemy tanks were only a few yards away. The 12th Field Artillery got more than 10 of the tanks for sure. A German officer who fought with the German Army in that area said the German officers and non-commissioned officers could not control their soldiers because of the American artillery. He claimed even the near misses disabled tanks by causing concussions to those operating the tanks. The 2nd Infantry Division made history for the United States, the U.S. Army, and for the division itself in those hard days of fighting. They left a legacy that will live forever in the U.S. Army and in military files. A German officer who fought in the Bulge said: "The 2nd Infantry Division did not know how to retreat."

The Battle of the Bulge did not end in Elsenborn. There was still the Siegried Line to be penetrated and the Rhine River to cross. On the Siegried Line the Germans were dug deep into the ground with tree logs and dirt as thick as 5 feet on top of them. Again, the situation called for many artillery rounds and TOT's to drive the Germans out of their bunkers and put them to retreat. Many of them did not go easy.

The next step was to cross the Rhine River. This action, too, called for artillery support. Information has it that 20,000 American casualties occurred during the Rhine River crossings. But then, victory on the battlefield is hardly ever cheap.

Of course, the Americans wanted to be the first to cross the river, and so did the British. It might be safe to say that General Patton's units were the first ones to make it across the Rhine. Our division crossed over on 21 March, shortly after midnight on a pontoon bridge constructed by the U.S. Army Engineers.

The last rough spot for the 2nd Infantry Division troops was Leipzig, a German stronghold. The American and British pilots called it Ack-Ack Alley. There were hundreds of anti-aircraft weapons positioned there. Hitler's youth was assigned to help defend Leipzig. There were even some German female soldiers defending the site.

The Second Division Artillery played a large, important role in the final capture of Leipzig. The stronghold was under siege from 13-19 April, when it was captured by the 2nd Infantry Division soldiers. From Leipzig the fighting was light. Germans soldiers were surrendering by the thousands to avoid capture by the Russian Army. The Germans wanted no part of the so-called Uncle Joe Stalin.

The other 28 divisions fought hard battles, too, but I do not know all the details of their battles in the Bulge. I am sure their story has been told by the responsible ones who fought with their divisions.

Sound military leadership, example by officers and enlisted leaders (against huge odds) got the job done and stopped the German Army in the Battle of the Bulge. There is no substitute for military leadership and discipline. The responsible ones must set an example if a huge task, like the Battle of the Bulge, is to be won. Well-disciplined and properly led soldiers are brave and will not cave in when the chips are down.

The Battle of the Bulge was not decided at Bastogne, nor at Elsenborn. It was decided as a result of a combined effort by the other 28 American Divisions who defeated the German troops in all the different battles that took place. When the Battle of the Bulge finally ended 45 days had passed. There were about 80,000 casualties, 15,000 frozen feet, and approximately 10,000 killed in the fighting.

Once the Battle of the Bulge was over and the Rhine River was crossed, the war in Europe was coming ever closer to an end. There was little time left for the wicked ones and their friends to drink booze from human skulls, or to use lamps with human skulls as lamp shades. The time was upon Adolph Hitler and 20 of his wicked human butchers (and their families) to start to make plans for self destruction. Some chose to change into civilian attire and vanish into the night. Fact was, their wicked practices and glory days were coming to an end, and they eventually did. Again the German people could display a friendly smile and stop calling the people of the world swine. War is hell, but it teaches fools a big plenty.

The Germans surrendered on 7 May 1945. On 8 May 1945 it became official with the signing of the Unconditional Surrender at Reims, Germany. Two pens were used, forming a "V" for victory. The signing at Reims officially ended WWII in Europe.

The 2nd Infantry Division ended up in Pilsen, Czechoslovakia. When it was announced that the war was over in Europe, the people could be heard crying from joy, laughing, singing and everything that could be thought of. The military men got a real good night of sleep for a change.

When the division moved from Pilsen, Czechoslovakia to LeHarve, France I could really see what war was all about. The Germans did a lousy job picking up their dead from the battlefield. It was so good to be an American in that war.

Shortly after the move to France, the division lost the high point personnel and had them replaced with low point personnel. The division had been picked to ship out to the Pacific to fight the Japanese and help bring an end to the war there.

The division arrived in the U.S. in July 1945 to prepare for the mission in the Pacific. There were only a small number of us in the battalion who elected to stay on with the division to fight in the Pacific. We were on 30-days furlough (now called leave) when the war in the Pacific ended. On 14 August, 1945, Japan accepted the terms of her surrender.

Upon the final surrender of the enemy in WWII, the United States of America and all Americans rejoiced along with the rest of the free world. Church bells were ringing, people were singing, dancing in the streets, drinking booze, and doing many other things (I cannot mention) because they were overjoyed. The war was finally over.

The world and its people were more than grateful to the United States of America and the American people for bringing an end to the WWII conflagration. Yes, our performance in WWII proved that the United States was in the driver's seat. Labels read: Made In America. The American people were (and still are) the best in the world. The U.S. Government in Washington was a small one then. It had to be to achieve the required efficiency in all aspects of operations. During WWII the government in Washington put the American people first, those stateside and the ones abroad. I wish we could have it that way now.

THE ARMY AIR CORPS

The Navy did a lot of training on the Texas coast while the Army was whipping them into combat readiness on land. The Army Air Corps was a large group and had to really get with the program to get ready for overseas action. They trained in fields and pastures. Texas was full of the Air Cadets and the planes they trained in. The State of Texas had many air bases in the WWII era.

The Texans welcomed them and were always proud of them. Many single women from Texas became Army Air Corps brides.

Don't let me leave out the value of rental property where service personnel were concerned. There was a severe shortage of rental properties, so even a good size chicken house rented well. That proved nothing could stop young love.

NOTES TO PONDER

In WWI the French wanted to use the United States troops as their replacements. General John Pershing told them firmly, "No. Give us the area and we will take our own objectives." General Pershing wanted the Americans to take credit for fighting the war for the United States. That was why the American troops were sent there.

We could have used General John (Black Jack) Pershing in the Battle of the Bulge to tell General Bernard Montgomery to commit the British troops to fight for their own objectives. He could have also instructed Montgomery to keep him informed on how well the British were performing on those objectives.

General Douglas MacArthur didn't have that problem in WWII in the Pacific. He was the commander and he assigned the areas and objectives. Everyone knew General MacArthur meant business and got with it.

Wars are political and the British wanted to make it look like they were the only ones who knew how to fight a war. Their real aim might have been to save the lives of their own troops in the Battle of the Bulge.

The Korean War was the first war the United States fought without securing a victory. Our troops are still sitting in Korea over 40 years later. The South Korean Government is putting Americans out of work because the South Koreans are making products to sell in America.

In the Vietnam War many Americans lost their lives and thousands were wounded, just for the American businesses to try to get a foothold in Vietnam. They finally succeeded 21 years later, again looking for cheap labor to put more Americans out of work.

What must the Americans do to receive fair recognition to fight in war(s) for this country?

The United States Army takes the brunt of the war, large or small. The war is never over until the infantry rifleman takes the last objective on the battlefield.

SURRENDER

Germany surrendered 7 May 1945 and signed the Unconditional Surrender on 8 May 1945. Two pens were used, forming a "V" for victory.

At the time of the German surrender the largest invasion of all invasions was being planned against Japan. The invasion was to be carried out 1 November 1945. Estimated casualties for the American Forces was 1,000,000, with 500,000 for the British. Acting as a reserve to follow up the initial assault was the First Army under the command of General Courtney Hodges. This army was to be re-deployed from Europe. Among its 11 divisions (1 airborne and 10 infantry) were some British units. The Second Infantry was one of them.

However, the atomic bomb became available for military use and President Harry S. Truman gave the "go ahead" to use it. In 1945, the first uranium bomb, called "Little Boy", was dropped on Hiroshima 6 August. The second atomic bomb, "Fat Boy", was released over Nagasaki on 9 August. This facilitated the Japanese surrender on 14 August 1945. On 2 September 1945 the Unconditional Surrender of Japan was signed aboard the U.S.S. Missouri in Tokyo Bay. Five pens were used. One went to General Wainwright, the second to General Percival, the third was presented to the United States Government Archives, and the fourth went to the U.S. Military Academy at West Point. The fifth pen, a small red one pulled by General MacArthur from his pocket, already belonged to Mrs. MacArthur. Yes, General MacArthur also signed the Instrument of Surrender.

THE NAVY AND THE BUILDUP IN EUROPE

The Navy had to fight its way through to get the cargo ships to Europe. The German U-boats and submarines were plentiful and sank many of the American cargo vessels. Although President Franklin D. Roosevelt gave the cargo vessels the order to shoot to kill, many of the ships were lost. The British had a good navy. The U.S. and the Brits finally got the best of the Germans in the cargo vessel struggle. In the end, the U.S. and British navies were the champs.

The Merchant Marines were tough all the way. The U.S. and

British navies rode shotgun for them. Many times the sailors had to sleep on steel decks.

The U.S. Marines made many invasions and did a lot of island hopping in the war. They were a good military organization, but at times a little too noisy for such a small branch of the service. There never was and never will be a light objective for the Marine Corps to deal with. All objectives are very difficult for them. The Sea Bees had it rough, but kept quiet and got the job done in fine fashion. Their main mission was centered in the Pacific. They are a proud outfit, earning their glory the hard way.

THE KOREAN WAR

25 JUNE 1950 - 26 JULY 1953
3 YEAR, 1 MONTH, 1 DAY

It was 4 years, 10 months, and 23 days since the conclusion of WWII. The gun smoke had barely vanished from the battlefields, sea, and sky. America was still drunk on the WWII victory. However, Josef Stalin (and his wicked staff of human butchers) hated to see the people comfortable, enjoying life in all aspects and the peace found throughout the world. So, on 25 June, 1950, he ordered an attack on South Korea by the North Korean Army to test the **will** and **guts** of the United States. The Russians were craving fresh blood for their battlefields. Their hearts held misery and suffering for the South Korean people. They fed on the hardship and disruption of the United States and the rest of the free world.

The Russian government did not commit one Russian soldier to the Korean War. They had the North Koreans and the Red Chinese puppets do their dirty work for them. This proved the Russians were a rattlesnake with a smile. It quickly became evident that the United States military won WWII with 100% support of the homefront, but the politicians had lost the struggle for peace.

The United States and United Nations Headquarters in New York had to act quickly after the North Korean Armed Forces crossed into South Korea. It was evident the South Korean Army was no match for the well trained and well armed North Korean troops. The President of the United States ordered General Douglas MacArthur (Supreme Allied Commander in Japan) to send the US Air Force and ground troops (from Japan) to South Korea.

The Korean War was labeled a "police action". That gave the

North Korean top military command, and later the Red China military command, the signal that they wouldn't be defeated on the battlefield. The Korean and Chinese troops quickly realized that morale in the American military ranks was hard to maintain because American military morale stems from permission for the fighting men to secure a victory on the battlefield. Playing hide-and-seek with weapons and live ammunition was a very difficult game to play.

The Joint Chiefs of Staff were directed to voice that the Korean War was in the wrong place at the wrong time. That rendered much comfort to the enemy, but none was felt by our fighting men. This caused the American soldiers plenty of dark patches before their eyes between the battlefield and Washington (and the United Nations Headquarters). Many would die in a war for nothing.

UNITED STATES TROOPS IN JAPAN

The American military troops stationed in Japan were not combat ready by any means. The military personnel shipped from stateside for assignment to Japan were not properly trained and the training ranges in Japan were not adequate to complete their training. There was a vast shortage of qualified personnel, as well as inadequate supplies and equipment.

The primary mission of the American troops stationed in Japan was occupation related, guard duty and sports. It was an assignment of leisure and fun. Furthermore, many of the military personnel were deeply in love with the Japanese women and were of little value to their units upon arrival to the battlefield. It took them a considerable amount of time to shake it. In military ranks that is called a "case of the sweet backside".

The Japanese Kitchen Police (KP) personnel knew more about the kitchen field ranges than did the American cooks. This fact became very evident on the battlefield.

The leisure and fun habits of the American troops came to a fast halt after June 25th. The old song sings: Time Changes Everything. A sense of urgency was put into full play. For the American WWII veterans, it was back to war again in less than five years.

THE 24TH INFANTRY DIVISION

The 24th Infantry Division was the first United States Army

division dispatched from Japan to repel the attacking North Korean forces in South Korea. Both officers and enlisted men had to be transferred from the other divisions based in Japan to bring the 24th to a more acceptable combat posture. It was a "rob Peter to pay Paul" type situation.

When the American troops of the 24th Infantry Division faced the enemy, they quickly learned that they were largely outnumbered and that the North Korean Army was combat ready and meant business. Many of the men were lost in just a few days in combat. Their Division Commander was captured by the enemy. It was not a good picture for the division.

This was the first time the United States military forces engaged the communists in a war. The going was very rough for the troops of the 24th Infantry Division and for all those who followed. It was hoped that once the American troops appeared in South Korea that the North Korean Armed Forces would turn tail and retreat to North Korea. Not so. Instead, the little rice snappers hung tough all the way. Their mind was closed to everything but the capture and takeover of South Korea. And they almost did it. The 24th Infantry Division (its fighting men) never received full credit for the superb job they did before reinforcements arrived.

THE 25TH INFANTRY DIVISION

Shortly after the 24th Infantry Division departed for South Korea the 25th Infantry Division was loaded onto Japanese trains. Rails were shined as a bluff to the enemy, but the North Korean Top Military Command paid no attention to it. And so the 25th Infantry Division was loaded onto Navy vessels and sailed for South Korea.

However, the arrival of the 25th Infantry Division was not enough. The 25th and what was left of the 24th Infantry Division were ordered to hold Pusan until help arrived.

THE PUSAN PERIMETER

The 65 holding days in Pusan were a very exciting period. The North and South Koreans looked very similar and spoke the same language. This made for a great deal of difficulty for the United States troops in the area.

In the daylight hours the North Koreans would change into civilian attire and pose as South Korean civilians. This enabled them to monitor the American forces and their positions. After dark the North Koreans traded their civilian clothing for military uniforms and gave the American Forces a full payload of hell.

The front lines were thinly held at best. The enemy went all-out to attack the American artillery firing battery positions in hopes to put the howitzers out of action or try to destroy them completely. This was a time when even the military chaplains found it safer to have a pistol on their hip rather than a prayer on their lips. It was a rough spot, but our fighting men kept it intact until help arrived.

During the 65 holding days of Pusan most of the replacements for combat units came from the South Korean Conscripts. This was difficult because the American soldiers spoke Korean no better than the conscripts spoke English. Finger pointing and body (sign) language worked fairly well in daylight, but were of little value in the dark. To add to the chaos, the Korean soldiers were not used to eating the U.S. Army field rations and were "loose as a goose" with upset stomachs for days on end.

The "can and will do" American attitude on the battlefield pulled us through. We all hung tough. Had it not been for the WWII Veterans, Pusan would not have been held.

THE INCHON INVASION

The Inchon Invasion saved the troops in the Pusan perimeter from being captured or completely destroyed. In August, all Commanders in the Pusan area were instructed to inform all the key personnel in their battalions that the situation, from a military standpoint, was a serious matter. There was a likening of the situation to that of Dunkirk during WWII in Europe and that all of the troops might not be able to get out safely.

The troops were also told that General MacArthur had a plan to save the fighting men from being destroyed but the people responsible in Washington were very much opposed to the plan. Even the United States Navy Top Command voiced against it, expounding that the plan was far too risky.

The hard-nosed general did not buy their gusts of excuses and told the Navy top brass "It appears that I have more faith in the Navy than the Navy has in itself!" The invasion troops were loaded on the ships, anchors raised, and the invasion was a complete success.

Meanwhile, all the other divisions had objectives assigned to them in the north and all these divisions reached them on time. This string of successes liberated South Korea. The American fighting forces and the South Korean forces and the entire South Korean nation rejoiced.

General MacArthur was the big hero, which he had every right to be. He used the Lord's Prayer for the liberation speech, which was somewhat unusual to many. The people in Washington and at the United Nations Headquarters in New York quickly jumped on the victory wagon. The morale of our fighting men curved straight up.

MILITARY INTELLIGENCE AND WAR PLANNING

Two British civilians were included in strategic meetings and were subsequently leaking secrets to the Russians. Many plans and other important information concerning the war went first through Russia, and were then forwarded with speed to the enemy top command for use against the United Nations Forces. This made it very difficult for the United Nations Headquarters in Tokyo to obtain full, successful results from such plans.

Once the headquarters in Tokyo caught on and reported their concerns to Washington, the two Brits beat it to Russia. That proved that civilians have no business participating in meetings and strategic planning concerning the fighting men in a war. Our fighting men took big beatings on the battlefields as a result of the blunders that stemmed from England.

It was also discovered that the British were selling materials to China; materials that proved to be very valuable to our enemies when used against the Americans in the war. England was supposed to be our friend and even called herself one of the "Big Three". Then again, Russia also considered herself to be one of the "Big Three". Both countries played America for a sucker and got away with it.

SHOOTING ON THE BATTLEFIELD

There was plenty of gunfire on the battlefield for the United States Army. For example, the light artillery batteries once fired over two thousand rounds of ammunition in a single night. This statistic was repeated many times throughout the war. It was needed simply to hold off the enemy. The American artillery soldiers fired more ammunition in the Korean War than they did in WWII in its entirety, whose total was up in the vast thousands.

The artillery soldier's job is to shoot. The infantry soldier's job seems to be to always take the brunt of the war. Good thing the military had the WWII hardware and equipment to fight with. It was well tested in combat and it functioned well for the fighting men. This was no place for junk. Further, it was also a blessing that there were no American military women to cope with. They could not have withstood the hardships of the severe battles or the natural elements. The fools who think that women can fight along side men, such as it was in that war, fail to realize that when God put a head on people that he did it for a purpose, not just to have a place to hang two ears.

PRESIDENT SYNGMAN RHEE OF SOUTH KOREA

President Rhee's loyalty to the United States and the Supreme Allied Commander (and all other commanders) was unquestionable. He maintained 100% loyalty at all times. He turned all his military forces over to the American commanders to use as they saw fit. His fighting men did the best they knew how in the war and performed admirably.

Word has it that it was good to have President Rhee around when discussions turned to the subject of American history. It was rumored that President Rhee knew more about American history than did most Americans. This fact really souped up the American soldiers and was another way President Rhee proved his undeniable loyalty to the United States.

THE UNITED STATES TOOK THE BRUNT OF THE WAR

Branch of Service	Number Serving	Battle Deaths	Other Wounds Deaths	Not Mortal
Army	2,834,000	27,704	9,429	77,596
Navy	1,177,000	458	4,043	1,576
Marines	424,000	4,267	1,261	23,744
Air Force	1,285,000	1,200	5,884	368
Totals	**5,720,000**	**33,629**	**20,617**	**103,284**

MAJOR CONTRIBUTIONS TO UN FORCES IN KOREA

In WWII the United States of America had 16,112,566 military personnel in uniform. Sixty-two percent of the entire US war effort went to the European Theater of Operations. England was the most vocal foreign nation crying for American help. But when the Korean War came along, England was not interested. South Korea was much too far away from home and a very poor country as well. England placed little importance in general where South Korea was concerned.

All the nations in Europe gladly took the American foreign aid during and after WWII. The European nations received more American military replacements during WWII than did South Korea during the Korean War. In WWII the British knew where all the light (weak) objectives were on the battlefield and were properly assigned to them. The British troops sent to South Korea brought plenty of good tents with them. The old saying goes: "A dry piece of bread is better than no bread at all."

During the Korean War the European countries furnished merely a drip-of-the-faucet type of support to the United States. See the chronological buildup of major units in Korea. See also the excerpts from the Military History in Washington, D.C.

THE THIRTY-EIGHTH PARALLEL WAR

The Thirty-Eighth Parallel was crossed October 8th. Red China had to know in advance that their homeland would not be attacked. Red China entered the war in November.

The first United States Army unit crossed the Thirty-Eighth Parallel October 8th and the other United Nations Forces followed. The North Korean forces quickly recoiled and sucked the UN Forces to the Manchurian Border by November 21st. This action drew Red China into the war.

The Chinese troops were well positioned. The Chinese soldiers executed their first massive attack on the UN Forces on November 26th. This made it a new war and the UN Forces found themselves largely outnumbered on the battlefield. Many of the UN Units found themselves trapped and surrounded by the Chinese troops.

The weather was bitterly cold with winds causing the temperatures to drop 75 degrees below zero. There were no (winter) garments available for issue to the troops at that time. It was a test of men. Frostbite, colds, fever, chills and pneumonia abounded. There was an insufficient number of medical personnel to properly care for the men, as well as a lack of medical supplies. Many of those brave men did not make it. Transportation, both air and ground, was totally inadequate to handle the heavy load of the sick and wounded. It certainly brought to mind that war is hell and that severe weather is the number one enemy on the battle-field.

A withdrawal was ordered for the UN troops, but it was not an easy withdrawal to accomplish. In order to withdraw many of the UN Forces had to fight their way out of Chinese encirclements. The enemy mined the mountain road passes, had their infantry soldiers set up strong road blocks, and placed troops with machine guns and mortars on high grounds to cut down the retreating UN Forces. A great deal of military hardware had to be abandoned when troops were ordered to "hoof it" to safety the best they could. Some were taken out of the area by waterways, which was not a Sunday afternoon fun cruise.

To further complicate the withdrawal of UN Forces, the North Korean military had laid large numbers of land mines throughout the North Korean countryside and along the roads. It was a good thing the Chinese lacked sufficient ground transportation to follow the retreating UN Forces. It would have been much worse than what it was. It was a big help when the Chinese soldiers (on foot) tired of pursuing the retreating UN Forces.

The Red Chinese Forces had it made because they fought the war from their backyard, knowing they would not be attacked by the UN Forces on Chinese soil. For example, one instruction allowed the UN Forces to bomb only half of the bridge separating North Korea and Manchuria (the half adjacent to North Korea). The US and UN pilots were not good enough to bomb half of a bridge out without irking the enemy.

Once the UN Forces regrouped and regained a suitable footing the war became like a poker game. Win today and give it back to the opponents tomorrow. It was a long, and sometimes rough, poker game. The wishful thinking, "Home by Christmas", was quickly put to an end. A rotation program and policy had to be worked out and was put to use for the troops in 1951. The mess sergeants often came through with coffee to warm the troops. "The coffee was pure as an angel, strong as love, black as the devil and hot as hell!"

CHRISTMAS DAY AND MAIL

Not all the troops had a turkey dinner on Christmas Day. Those who did often had their meal interrupted by the enemy, wounding many and killing some. When the area was infested with enemy mines and the physical enemy was not far away, the type of dinner (feeding) offered is called muzzle loading. Their chow instructions were to eat their meal as quickly as possible and return to their battle positions.

The mail did not catch up with the fighting men for a long time after the Chinese entered the war. Their comment was "Better alive than mail". When the mail did finally catch up with the fighting men, it was well appreciated.

THE MILITARY DOCTORS AND NURSES

As in WWI and WWII the doctors and nurses in the military had a bloody job to do. Adequate (sincere) thanks and appreciation can never be expressed to them for the excellent job they performed. The military nurses are women of tempered steel. Bloody tasks and long hours couldn't stop them. Those who have departed...may God rest their souls.

BEER FOR THE TROOPS ON THE BATTLEFIELD; ONE BEER PER DAY PER MAN

The American beer companies thought it would be good for morale (a spirit lifter) for the troops on the battlefield to have access to beer after a hard day's work. However, some of the pallor complexioned (tenderfoot) American mothers did not think so. The mothers justified their protests by saying the beer would change their sons to drunkards.

The Supreme Allied Commander and the officer and enlisted leaders ignored the mothers' protests because they thoroughly understood that one beer per day per man would not change the mama's boy from Sweet Little Willie to a Big Bad Bill. Those who did not want to drink the beer didn't have to. The availability of beer to the troops continued.

THE DRAFT FOR MILITARY SERVICE AND DIVORCES

As always, the rich kids became too important to die in a war. Therefore, the poor boys carried the war burden in the Korean War as they did in previous wars participated in by the United States of America. And divorces: The pastures to some became very green.

NO BATTALION OR DIVISION BOOKS FOR THE FIGHTING MEN IN KOREA

In WWII battalion and division books were issued to the military personnel upon conclusion of the war. The issue of these books to the fighting men is impossible when there is no victory in the battlefield. Even though victory was denied our fighting men, they still gave it their best shot to make the United States of America look as good as possible.

Military duty in peace and war can be compared with God's rains. God rains equally on the good and the wicked. The United States military does not sort out the good and the bad. They defend the entire nation as a whole.

The United States of America and all good Americans are still very proud of our fighting men in Korea for a job well done under less than desirable conditions. Even though victory was denied them, these men retain their spirit and pride. They are a very sad group of veterans, but are never ashamed. The United States Government in Washington is responsible for the well deserved monument earned by the Korean War veterans.

Not one American should be made to die in a war for nothing. The United States Military could have won the Korean War. The politicians shot America in the foot on this one and America (Big Mom) has been painfully limping ever since.

The United States received very little help from Europe in the Korean War. The following is a breakdown of support received from foreign nations during the Korean War:

UNITED KINGDOM: 1 RAF Unit; 9 Naval Vessels;
    1 Brigade Group; 1 Brigade
 FRANCE: 1 March Battalion
 GREECE: 6 C-47 Type Airplanes; 1 Infantry Battalion

CANADA:1 C-54 Type Airplane Squadron; 3 Destroyers;
1 Brigade; Canadian Pacific Airlines
NETHERLANDS:1 Destroyer; 1 Infantry Battalion
TURKEY: First Turkish Forces Command Brigade
BELGIUM: 1 Infantry Battalion
AUSTRALIA: 1RAAF Fighter Squadron; 2 Destroyers;
2 Infantry Battalions
SOUTH AFRICA: 1 Fighter Squadron
LUXEMBOURG: 1 Infantry Detachment
THAILAND: 1 Corvette; C-47 Type Airplanes;
1 Infantry Battalion; 1 Troop Transport
INDIA: Field Ambulance Unit
PHILIPPINES: 1 Battalion Combat Team; 17 Tanks
DENMARK: Hospital Ship; 1 Motor Ship
NEW ZEALAND: 1 Frigate; 1 Artillery Battalion
SWEDEN: Field Hospital
COLUMBIA: 1 Frigate; 1 Infantry Battalion
NORWAY: Mobile Hospital; 1 Cargo Ship
ETHIOPIA: 1 Infantry Battalion
ITALY: Field Hospital
PANAMA: Free access to the Panama Canal

A WAR WITHOUT VICTORY

It always favors the enemy.
Life on the battlefield becomes very cheap.
Respect for the mothers of the fighting sons is at a very low ebb.
It allows half-assed Americans to support the enemy.
Prisoners are left in enemy hands to rot.
It divides the country.

The reason I was able to write the material on the Korean War is because General Douglas MacArthur saved the troops in the Pusan Perimeter from capture and destruction by the North Korean Army. It was a very close call.

THE VIETNAM WAR 1964 - 1973

THE FAUCET DRIPPED SINCE 1954
All wars are dumb and stupid. But a war without victory is totally dumb and totally stupid.

It was the American businessmen who instigated the Vietnam War and made sure it would be a very long war. The businessmen couldn't have cared less about the nation and its people, the fighting men and their families, the mothers of the fighting men, the prisoners of war who were left behind in the enemy countries to rot.

These businessmen have never been seen or heard praying over the graves of fallen soldiers nor have they been seen visiting the wounded troops in hospitals or comforting the families of the soldiers that did not make it back alive. These rich "biggies" could care less.

THE UNITED STATES MILITARY RESERVES

The United States Military Reserves "howled" themselves out of going to Vietnam to fight. They did not want to leave their families, jobs, schools, or even the states. And they knew all the right people in Washington. So instead of using the reserves, the draft was increased.

The reserves made it sound like the draftees were all bullet proof when, in fact, they were not. The reservists made it appear that the draftees wouldn't be harmed by leaving their families, jobs, schools and their states. The families of the draftees did not know how to manipulate the Big Boys in Washington like the reservists did. The draftees got a deep shafting in the Vietnam War.

The mothers and wives of the Vietnam veterans have yet to be thanked for providing those veterans for combat duty. Many of the soldiers did not come back alive and some were left behind to rot in enemy hands as prisoners of war.

When the Reserves and Guard were not called up for duty during Vietnam it compelled the American working class (taxpayers) to fund two military payrolls: one for the Reserves and Guard and one for the draftees.

Yes, in wartime, it pays to know the Big Boys in Washington.

THE AMERICAN NEWS MEDIA

There were good ones and there were bad ones in the news media throughout the Vietnam War era. They all should have been made to fight for the news with the men fighting the war.

Most of the journalists would have wiped their rear ends with the First Amendment if they had been made to fight for the news. On many occasions their silver tongues would have been silent.

The less than reputable journalists kept the enemy clued as to what information he was unable to obtain for himself. These journalists need not look around; they know who they are.

THE PEACE TALKS

In a war where the fighting is not going just right for the enemy, the enemy will often agree to peace talks in an effort to get caught up in his areas of deficiency. The United States and the South Vietnamese Forces in Vietnam had a very favorable situation going until an elected official in Washington instigated the peace talks. Of all places, Paris, France was chosen as the site for the talks. The French had suffered great losses in Vietnam themselves.

The official that instigated the peace talks was deficient on military knowledge. He had spent only a short time in the US Navy Reserves. The only military experience he possessed was how to duck bird droppings in his weekend training with the reserves.

During the peace talks period, the United States Military should have been given orders to hit the enemy with all the fire power available to them at the time. This would have let the enemy know the United States of America meant business in everything it does. Instead, the enemy was informed that the US would only attack on certain days and specific places. For that blunder the South Vietnamese later lost the war.

At the time of the peace talks, little more than 20 years had passed since the United States military had whipped Germany and Japan, two of the most wicked and powerful enemies in the world. Now, they were being denied permission to whip a small number of rice snappers in Vietnam. The world is still laughing at the United States for this today.

If the spirit, pride and glory of the United States are to be properly maintained, there can be no substitute for victory in the course of war. Americans never have, and never will, enjoy taking a back seat in anything they do. During the Vietnam War this was forced upon them.

WHEN MILITARY PERSONNEL WERE RETURNING HOME AND THE FINAL RETURN HOME FROM THE WAR

Many Vietnam veterans were spat on by half-assed Americans who failed to realize the veterans didn't go to Vietnam by their own choice. Most of the Vietnam veterans were ordered to war by the United States Government in Washington. They should have been spitting on the Washington establishment instead. Many of those being harassed were draftees who did not volunteer to go to Vietnam.

When I returned from Vietnam in 1966, I was approached by two men and two women. They came up to me and said: "The United States Military personnel are murderers in Vietnam!" I gave them the straight answer that "The United States Military does not ask you to go to war, therefore, you should be directing your unqualified spicy remarks at those responsible in Washington." All of them sprightly beat it.

My encounter proved how little truth most American civilians really knew about the United States military operations whether in peace or in war. The country at that time had many Americans who trotted all over the States trying to get Americans to work against the involvement in Vietnam. The schools were their primary targets. Some students took it upon themselves to protest the war effort. Some carried it a little too far and lost their lives for their cause.

The United States of America needs a policy stating that not one American will be drafted to fight in a war that does not include an effort for victory for the troops. Not one American mother should be made to provide a son or daughter to die for nothing in a war like we had in Vietnam.

When the shameful war (in Vietnam) was finally called off, not one elected official or American businessman stepped forward to claim responsibility for the Vietnam War. Politicians only crave the sweet, and leave the bitter to others. The big businessmen could have cared less because they had already made their profits.

It's a good thing the military teaches their troops how to take the bitter with the sweet. Most of the personnel were able to ignore the fools who were insulting them for doing their duty for their country.

The old song sings: "There are dark clouds in the sky, but there will be blue skies again". The words in the old song pulled many military personnel through. Even though victory was denied them and they were sad, they were not ashamed.

I was a regular army soldier and it was my duty to be there. The Guard and Reserve units also had a duty and should have been used to the fullest extent. There were many regular army soldiers left in the states to warm chairs and sip coffee. The draftees should have been the last ones to be sent to the Vietnam War. It sure didn't happen this way.

The North Vietnamese are still using the American prisoners of war as poker chips to gain favorable trade agreements and it appears that they are being given the opportunity to win. Of course, the American businessmen will do anything for money. But then again, they have no sons in North Vietnam rotting as prisoners of war.

The United States and most of the foreign nations used pretty much the same strategic operations in Vietnam. Only the South Koreans fought the war like it should have been fought, without interference from politicians and the media. The United States of America and the good American people are still hanging their heads in shame because of the Vietnam War; the way it was fought and the way it ended. A person only has one life to live and should not be ordered to give it up for nothing.

THE ADVISOR MISSION

The United States Government in Washington failed to ascertain how much the South Vietnam Government would do on its own to make the policy and programs (agreed upon) work. Would they sort out the Vietcong from the South Vietnamese people? They did not.

The defeat of the Vietcong was the responsibility of the South Vietnamese Government, not that of the American Forces. Instead of defeating the Vietcong, the South Vietnamese top government went into living high on the hog. They allowed their people to continue to hang onto the sestas. Instead of getting with the program the American way, the officials sent out beggars and dope pushers in full force.

The advisors' (sent to South Vietnam) hands continued to be tied. "The mission will fail unless Washington demands maximum results from the South Vietnamese" was the writing on the wall. The advisor's mission was a failure. They were sent to South Vietnam to do a job. Instead of getting their job done, they spent their time begging the South Vietnamese Government to go along with the American type training.

GENERAL DOUGLAS MACARTHUR

President Lyndon B. Johnson asked General MacArthur for his views and wisdom on whether or not the United States should be committed in the Vietnam War. General MacArthur's answer was "no".

MacArthur knew that it would be another war fought without a victory. He knew that without victory (with loss of lives for nothing) the United States of America and the fighting men would be put to shame again.

General MacArthur's views were ignored. Again, the politicians would win.

PROPAGANDA

A vast buildup of American Troops in Vietnam hinged on a full payload of propaganda. Only a few American military personnel were killed by the Vietcong, but those in charge were not willing to let the Vietcong go unchallenged for it.

Our enemy in Vietnam had very small boats and little boats must always keep near shore. That's exactly what they did. However, to get into the war, those in charge made it appear as though the Vietcong and the North Vietnamese forces would invade American shores at any time.

Once the American Armed Forces were committed to combat, victory was denied them. The enemy knew all too well the hard talk. They also knew that easy fallbacks would be practiced when the chips were down, like it was in the Korean War. That's precisely what happened.

PLANNING AND FIGHTING OF THE WAR

The military star rank officers were almost left out of the war. Civilians, wearing civilian attire, took over the war operations. The Secretary of Defense became their dispatch clerk, coordinating personnel, equipment, hardware and supplies.

Word has it that the Army Chief of Staff had to work his way through about 250 civilian rubbernecks to get to see the President.

The skills of the civilians did not match those with military knowhow. Much confusion abounded. Their policies were about as sound as froth on water.

SCAPEGOATS

In a war without victory a scapegoat is usually picked (well in advance) to use when things go wrong. In the Vietnam War there were some general officers as commanders who were demoted. They lost their military careers because of their actions; actions that might have saved a few American lives on the battlefield.

War is a dirty business, but a war without victory is doubly dirty. The South Vietnamese Government would not remove its people from the battle area. These civilians could kill the Americans troops, but the American troops could not defend themselves by killing the civilians. What a way to fight a war, especially for a nation like the United States of America.

In the Korean War the government tried to use General Douglas MacArthur as a scapegoat. The government was vastly fooled (100%) because MacArthur took his case to the American people. As a result, many were booted out of Washington in the next election. One of MacArthur's kind could have been used in Vietnam. He always put America and its people, as well as the fighting men under his command, first and foremost in his actions.

I don't think that MacArthur would have made trips from Vietnam to a Texas ranch to teeth barbecue and to down drinks with the President. To MacArthur, this was an insult to the troops. Yes, there was plenty of room in Vietnam for a MacArthur type.

EXCESSIVE DRIFT FROM STATESIDE

Visits by political dignitaries to the battlefields were merely for the personal gain of the politicians. Those visits were a huge pain in the butt for the Top Commanders. The enemy did not call off the war so these politicians could fly over battlefields, looking out the plane windows. Their actions tended to aggravate an already tense situation for the Top Commanders.

A war is not fought with vote hunters or with those angling for a personal gain. Yes, the drift from stateside was very excessive to say the least. Those guilty of these actions need not look around; you know who you are.

ON THE BUILDUP IN 1965

There must have been a reason for the buildup in 1965, but it was evident there were more military personnel in the rear echelon that there were fighting the enemy on the front lines. In WWII only 20% of the total personnel was accounted for by rear support personnel.

Holding ground that has been taken would have been a good job for the personnel assigned to the rear. The military personnel in the rear assignments had it made all the way. Some of them were actually fattening up in their jobs. The taxpayers should not have to support soldiers to have it nice during wartime. In the case of the rear assignments, the taxpayers did.

Those of us who fought in WWII and Korea could not understand the moves. There was plenty of eye rolling and some lip biting from us.

FIGHTING THE WAR

The Americans on the battle sites did not know who the enemy was and, subsequently, often gave the enemy a second chance to stay alive. Because of strict instructions from Washington, they could not fire on the enemy first. The North Vietnamese and the Vietcong troops had no such instructions to hamper their war efforts. They fired first and asked questions later.

For example: The Special Forces had a barbershop in their headquarters area. During the buildup in 1965, this particular area was ordered to construct temporary helicopter pads using stones. The local barbershop owner put in her bid to furnish the stones for the helicopter pad construction. She was not awarded the contract. That very night enemy mortar fire hit the area. The Americans had no choice but to award her the contract, or have their hair trimmed with enemy mortar shrapnel. Yes, in this war the enemy was very difficult to identify.

SEARCH AND DESTROY MISSIONS

The enemy could see the American and South Vietnamese troops coming at him. The enemy, on the other hand, had to be flushed out of the thick foliage to be seen and was often over-looked. The enemy knew many missions of the American troops were the hit and leave type. His nose thumbing continued at the American and South Vietnamese troops. The soldiers who did the fighting in the Vietnam War did the best they were permitted to do, but it was to no avail.

The air division and helicopter type fighting was about the only effective procedure that could be used in the Vietnam War. But winning in the morning only to give the captured area back to the enemy later in the day was no way to defeat the enemy. The ground recaptured by the enemy was often retained by him, and this made for an effective type of strategy for the enemy. Fighting for the same ground over and over quickly tired the American troops.

BRIEFINGS AND WEATHER FORECASTS

The briefings (concerning enemy troop status) were very hard on the enemy, or so the intelligence briefer claimed. Had their numbers been correct, the Vietcong and North Vietnamese would all have been killed in the first six months of combat in the Vietnam War. Those of us who fought in WWII and the Korean War knew that the briefings were much too hauty.

Two Air Force captains gave the weather briefings and forecasting. I asked them one day what kind of instruments they were using for the weather information gathering. Their answer was that they got their information from the South Vietnamese and the South Vietnamese have no weather instruments. They never missed.

THE DESERT WAR

It took the United States military too long to get to the Middle East to move in on what turned out to be a rabbit shoot. However, once the military got going, they were doing quite well. Then they received the command from Washington to stop the fighting. This command only produced another unsettled effort for America.

There was a shortage of water transportation to get our troops to the desert. This was the first time the United States Army had to hitchhike to war. Some of the seagoing transportation had to be furnished by the foreign nations. Charts and selected phrases do not ready troops for combat.

The Desert War was also the first time that the United States sent American military women to war with the male personnel. Many of the women were displeased to find they had to share their living quarters and latrines with the men. Well, they asked for it by their own cackling when they claimed they could fit with the men in all aspects of military operations. In field duty and combat operations there are bare butts and other private parts to be seen. There is no other way the military can function in those operations. A combat situation also calls for plain and to the point language, which is not always pleasing to a woman's ears. Men do not have time during field operations to worry about providing private conditions for the women. In addition to this, the women's fighting capability is not such that the United States military could not fight a war without them. The short stint in the Middle East surely proved that female personnel would do better in assignments such as those found in hospitals, finance, and any duty other than that of combat field duty.

We do not hear the military nurses recommending that military women be assigned to combat units. These nurses have first-hand knowledge that the battlefield is no place for women. These nurses have the bloody job of caring for the wounded and dying as a result of combat duty.

God created women to offer comfort, preserve life (not destroy it), and to enforce safety where possible. Furthermore, He had his own mother to act as a model for other women to emulate. We never see pictures of Mary wearing military fatigues and armed with a rifle.

Compare the United States Armed Forces with a professional ball club. We do not see women playing professional sports with men because they well know that the game, when played with men, is too much for them. We do not hear the sports announcer saying, "Pitching for the New York Yankees today is Polly Smith and she is six months pregnant. Catching today is Sally Jones and she is eight months pregnant. Playing second base and short stop are the Parker sisters, both in their ninth month. Sue Johnson on third base (not pregnant) will have to really hustle to cover for all the others." Women in the outfield would be afraid to bounce off the wall behind them because they might get hurt. This would be a lousy game, at best, to watch.

Keep in mind that sports are only a game played for fun. The defense of our nation is very serious business and there is no place for the women in combat units. Period. Sports people can lose in the fall and return next spring to try again. The United States military forces cannot lose on the battlefield and return for another try.

A good example for keeping women out of combat units is the Battle of the Bulge. In December, 1944, the Division Commander committed the headquarters personnel (the chair strength) to battle where they engaged the Germans in hand to hand combat. Had the personnel been women we would have been in trouble. As a result of the fighting men, the division held its position until help arrived.

Our United States Military Academies have been ordered to allow women to enter them as cadets. Now, other military type academies are being pressured to allow women to enroll in them as well. The standards at our military academies had to be lowered to a shameful level to accommodate the female cadets. The physical training standard was the first to be changed so the female cadet could compete. Many others had to be changed to please the softer side of the military ranks. Our military academies were designed to train men for battle. The United States Armed Forces is not a civilian type daily operation. Our military personnel are sworn in to handle all aspects of operations, light or heavy, dry or wet, hot or cold. These soldiers must be able to perform their duties for thirty hours without a break if need be. On the battlefield they must be able to fill in for others in addition to their own duties. The men cannot cry for their mothers when they are on the battlefield. Let's not forget there are invasions to be made by our military forces during war, and there are days each month a woman has to stay dry because of her monthly period.

If the required efficiency of our military is to be maintained, women must be kept out of the United States combat units.

Another example should be kept in mind. My own son was in the U.S. Air Force for four years, stationed on an Air Force base. Every time a big storm was closing in on the base the female personnel, both officer and enlisted, were transported out of the area to safety. Nothing more needs to be said.

The American news media needs to brush up on military knowledge and over-all military operations before they start to lip it big that the military women could do well in combat unit assignments. For example, in the Panama skirmish, a female captain assigned to a Military Police company was shown on TV and in the newspapers supposedly leading the military women into combat. A Military Police company is not an infantry rifle company! Military Police personnel are responsible for law and order, controlling traffic, and making sure no one steals the General's wife. They do not fight wars.

The news media also asked the First Lady if the military women should be assigned to combat units. Her answer was something like "In some cases." This answer was nothing more than vote hunting for husband's next election. My own wife heard the First Lady's answer and said, "There is yet another one who doesn't know her butt from a hole in the ground when it comes to assigning women in the military." My wife served with the military in WWII. She stands by her claim that women have no business in assignments with male personnel. At our house we tell it like it is.

An all out effort should be made to put the American feminist type women in the military service to train them to lead combat units, doing all the tasks required of our male personnel to get the job done. Also, we should form all female units; one infantry, artillery, tank, signal, and combat engineer battalion. Give the female personnel their own messhall and maintenance shops. That should do away with all their whining about women being permitted to serve with combat troops. This would prove that the women should not be permitted to serve on the battlefields.

In the event of war, employ the female personnel in an all female unit with Patricia Schroeder in command of all of them. There would be a news flash that Schroeder called a cease fire so the military mothers could change their babies' diapers, wipe their tears, and perform maintenance on the baby buggies. She would quickly learn that the enemy opposing her "troops" are not armed with lipsticks for rifles, powder puffs for hand grenades, nor bowls of jello for land mines.

The ones who think women should be in combat units must have been born under the bed. There are an unpredictable number of military operations in both war and peace time.

It's a good thing that women were not permitted to be assigned with combat troops in WWII. The military trained over 16 million men for combat to fight and win the war. There were no free rides in the military ranks back then. Man is war and was created to do hard work and women created to perform the lighter tasks.

There is also the problem of military women becoming pregnant and the time and money lost because of the pregnancy. American taxpayers are forced to fund the pregnancies of female military personnel. If the military women can have a baby at the government's expense, then all American women should have the United States government pay their bills and wages when they have a child as well. Female military pregnancies are very costly and it's just not worth the taxpayer's money.

Married women in the military can claim their husbands as a dependent. This is less than a joke for the U.S. Government to allow this to continue. There is no shortage of male personnel for the military service of this country. Let's not let these young bucks get a free ride as a dependent in the military from now on.

There is also far too many married junior enlisted personnel in the military today. This is very costly to the military and nation. The dependents outnumber the active duty personnel by a large number. The military needs to go back to like it was before WWII. The junior enlisted had to obtain permission from their commander to get married, or have at least three stripes on their sleeves. There were few married personnel in the military back then.

The American taxpayers are paying the bills for our military personnel. Let's clean up the military ranks so the taxpayers can be proud of the military forces again.

My statements on women in the military should not be construed as a personal dislike for women. In fact I like women very much. Women are a very important people, with the mothers the most important ones, not only in the United States, but throughout the entire world. Women provide the children that grow up to be our work force and our military forces. A woman never retires because her tasks and responsibilities are such that they never leave her regardless of age.

A good woman is like the fence posts that all wires are attached to. A good woman knows her place in life. Good women are rarely in the wrong place at the wrong time. They know how to sort out the dos and don'ts. They love their children and husbands. They know safety and know that women have no place in combat units.

Yes, I love women because the old song sings: I love the women and I love them all the same.

THE UNITED STATES OF AMERICA IN WARS

War/Conflict	Number Serving	Battle Deaths	Other Deaths	Wounded Not Mortal
Revolutionary War 1775-1783	?	4,400	?	6,000
War of 1812 1812-1815	286,700	2,200	?	4,500
Mexican War 1846-1848	78,700	1,700	11,500	4,100
Civil War 1861-1865	2,213,300	140,400	224,000	281,800
Spanish War	306,700	385	2,000	1,600
World War I 4 April 1917 11 Nov 1918	4,734,900	53,400	63,100	204,000
World War II 7 Dec 1941 31 Dec 1945	16,112,500	291,557	113,800	670,846
Korean Conflict 25 Jun 1950 27 Jul 1953	5,720,000	33,600	20,600	103,200
Vietnam Conflict 4 Aug 1964 27 Jan 1973	8,744,000	47,200	10,400	153,300

*Figures listed are approximate totals for that category.

WWII had to be won or we would not have the United States of America today. There were 433 Congressional Medals of Honor earned in WWII. Only 190 of the recipients survived to have the medals placed around their necks. Only 19 men have won the medal twice. Total number of medals awarded in all wars: 3,398. First Lt.

Bernard J.D. Irwin was the first recipient of the Congressional Medal of Honor, awarded to him on 14 February 1861. The Congressional Medal of Honor is now called simply the Medal of Honor.

If there were no American mothers, there would be no one to fight the wars or to keep America afloat. They are long overdue for a warm thank you from all of us. They are the most important people in America. They receive no awards for their untiring efforts.

AMERICA AND THE WORLD REJOICED

For the United States the war lasted 3 years, 8 months, and 25 days. To start from almost nothing and then accomplish what we did certainly proved that where there is unity there is strength. Hard work and plenty of savvy got the job done.

Upon the troops' return to the United States from the war in Europe, in July, 1945, there was a large crowd waiting for them in New York Harbor with a band playing. All the girls looked pretty, but the most beautiful of all was the Statue of Liberty. When these men returned home, the people paid for their drinks and food. They were world heroes.

FREEDOM AND PEACE: THE NEED TO PROTECT

No one knows the value of the country and flag, the value of life and freedom, and the value of our way of life better than the men who have fought in wars to preserve them. The United States military forces do not ask to go to war. The military personnel pray for peace because they are the ones who will be shot at. Young men get killed in war. The biggest losers in a war are:

Those killed in battle, The mothers and families of those killed, The wives and children of those killed.

This is why all the graves of all the young men are always saturated with sadness. They are so young when they die. These young men are the real heroes. The cemeteries they are resting in are so quiet and peaceful that one can almost feel and hear the grass grow around their graves. The white crosses want to tell that they have been driven into the ground with their mothers' hearts.

Over 40 years later, as he stood between their graves on Normandy Beach, President Reagan choked. Don't forget them. Remember them. Remember them with pride.

WARS ARE STUPID - WARS ARE DUMB:
A PERSONAL VIEWPOINT

Too many people today lack the military knowledge to fully realize what happens when war is forced upon the United States. They seem to think that the First Sergeants, and the Naval Chiefs of equal rank, are ordered to go to towns and cities, load men into trucks, and head off to war.

Wars are products of heads of government who do not believe in God and have no respect for human life. They do not practice the belief that where there is the spirit of God, one will find liberty and peace.

The military forces won WWII with 100% (plus) support from the home front. The politicians lost the peace in a shuffle.

Those responsible for the retired military personnel need to listen up. This is no time to pick the pockets of our active duty armed forces and our veterans, some still suffering from combat wounds. It is no time to ignore the mothers whose sons and daughters gave their lives in battle for their country.

The only way to prevent another large scale war is to be ready to repel the enemy at any time. This will save many thousands of lives. Peace is not free, or cheap. Let us all be proud and appreciate our active duty Armed Forces because they have a tough task to fulfill. There are no 8-hour schedules for the military because the military oath says so.

Disarmament talks, thus far, have accomplished very little. The strongest water in the world is the tear in a mother's eye. Why not include (in these talks) a mother and a wife from each country throughout the world who have lost a son or husband in a war. They could tell it at the meeting table like it really is - that wars are completely dumb and totally stupid. Their tears at these meetings just might do more than all the nuclear weapons threats in the entire world will ever do towards peace in the world.

The atomic bombs dropped on Japan does not bother me one bit. It hurts me like hell when I think of all the Americans who were killed at Pearl Harbor.

DISABLED VETERANS IN AMERICA

The disabled veterans have been short-changed in this country. They have to fight so hard for what little medical care they do receive. The personnel used to care for veterans should themselves be veterans. Using the same personnel that treated the wounded in combat would give the caregivers the needed perspective to adequately care for our veterans.

Currently many of our disabled veterans continually get the "runaround" and can not get any care without enlisting the help of their Congressmen. Our veterans should not have to go through that. The Veterans of Foreign Wars and the American Legion have been fighting very hard for the benefit of disabled veterans. This should not be necessary either. Too often the "job" is not getting done for our disabled veterans, with the problem being evident in every conflict since WWI.

To correct the problems of our disabled veterans I suggest the President, Secretary of Veterans Affairs, and the Secretary of Defense make a visit, one-on-one for eye contact, with the disabled veterans. This is the only way for them to learn firsthand if the veterans have been receiving the kind of care they earned while on the battlefield.

Many of our disabled veterans were draftees and did not volunteer to go to war. They were ordered to battle by the United States Government. They were called upon to serve their country and they did not let their country down. It is obvious that their (the veterans) government is the one letting them down.

Many disabled veterans were wounded by the very countries that are now receiving (just for the asking) American foreign aid. Yet, these same veterans must continually fight for what little care and support is available for them. It is fortunate that the Veterans of Foreign Wars organization has not caved in on their long, continuous fight for the disabled veterans. The American Legion has done a superb job of fighting for the disabled veterans as well. This is a never ending battle for the Veterans of Foreign Wars, the members of the American Legion, and the disabled veterans themselves.

MEMORIAL DAYS AND VETERANS DAYS

The elected officials in Washington are supposed to set an example for the nation to follow on Memorial Day and Veterans Day. We have not been seeing this. To correct this problem we should hold the championship rodeo contests in Washington, D.C. on Memorial Day and Veterans Day. The cowboys should rope the Washington officials and hold them long enough for the buglers to sound taps. No official should be excused from the events. Of course, the cowboy that ropes the largest number of officials successfully would win first prize.

Since the Korean and Vietnam wars the ceremonies on Memorial Day and Veterans Day have suffered from lack of attendance. Only a few flags can be seen flying on these holidays, as well as on June 14. That certainly proves what war without victory can do to a nation.

Making the American flag readily available just prior to these holidays might help to boost the American spirit of respect for these holidays. We would certainly have nothing to lose by making the effort.

Let's not forget this proven fact. The American flag and the United States military uniforms are the two most recognizable items in our nation and throughout the world. We cannot continue to scuttle them. Those who died fighting wars for the United States deserve better from us all.

CLOSING THE MILITARY COMMISSARY SYSTEM

The justification in Washington for the closing of the military commissary system appears to be that there is about $1 billion loss in them per year. We see nothing about Mexican nationals and other foreigners who are not American citizens who are costing American taxpayers at least $35 billion per year. We see nothing about the American taxpayers paying $1 billion in interest on the $4 trillion debt created in Washington by the big careless spenders. We see nothing on how the elected ones in Washington will use taxpayers money to pay for the $140 billion S&L blunder. By comparison to other big money expenditures, the $1 billion loss per year in the operation of the military commissary system is merely one lost feather from the duck's tail. Furthermore, since the conclusion of WWII, tons of money has been taken out of this country in the form of foreign aid with nothing in return.

This is not an accusation, but the commissary foodstuff have no hands and legs. For example: A German national who operated a post exchange for the Americans in Germany once asked my opinion on how to reduce losses in the store. My advice to him was to have a "shakedown" of workers on the way out after work. Sure enough, the first woman on her way out was wearing 11 pairs of underpants and had eight bras strapped to her legs. All the other employees had small items in their purses.

The pilferage in the civilian sector is much greater than that in the commissaries. So take your pick. The losses in the commissary system are being pointed out by the civilian businesses in hopes to have the commissary sales money to drop into their cash registers instead of those sales staying on the military installations where they belongs.

The commissaries are a must for the junior married personnel in the military forces. Their personal appearance costs many dollars per month for them. Many of them have to drive long distances to go home for vacations, holidays, and emergencies.

To put out the fire, I strongly suggest that all the active duty and the military retiree personnel write their Commander-In-Chief, President Bill Clinton or their congressman:

President Bill Clinton
The White House
Washington, D.C. 20500
Telephone: 1-202-456-1414

Member of Congress
The Honorable (Full Name of Congressman)
The House of Representatives
Washington D.C. 20515
Telephone: 1-202-224-3121

The military active duty and the military retirees and the old folks on Social Security are always the ones to be hit the hardest by the money hunters in Washington. The commissary privileges were <u>earned</u> in peacetime and in war. If we have no veteran we will not have a United States of America.

PRISONERS OF WAR

Prisoners of war are the responsibility of the President of the United States and the Secretary of State. It is believed that there are prisoners of war from WWII, and the Korean and Vietnam wars still in captivity. The exact number is unknown. Information has it that the Russians (Russkies) have control over them.

Since the end of WWII the United States government in Washington has been greasing the palms of the Russians. They have helped the Russians in many aspects since the WWII reconstruction. Since the wicked reign of Josef Stalin, who was called "Uncle Joe", the Russians have taken everything and given nothing. We are posting slow learners in Washington, D.C. to represent us, and they continue to let the Russians do the same as they always have.

Hearings in Washington continue to be held on the status of prisoners of war that were left behind. These hearings are not solving the problems of the prisoners of war. The chairman of the committee is showing little promise of getting them home and is at a loss to provide the family members with a straight answer. Patience is wearing thin concerning these family members. Some family members have passed on while waiting for answers. Meanwhile, the chairman continues to adjust his glasses, producing little or no results.

Retired military personnel have been dispatched to North Vietnam in an effort to learn where American soldiers were buried and to locate the whereabouts of live prisoners of war. These same military personnel were denied a victory on the battlefield. It is ironic that they should be assigned tasks that will cover the bases for the ones responsible for the lack of victory.

Since the conclusion of WWII, the United States has had 10 presidents in office. Not one of these presidents has been able to bring our prisoners of war home. The Secretary of State is very cool about it, with little being heard from him. It took a serious fight, one fought by a Texan, just to get the information on the prisoners of war made available to their families and nation.

Men have been running for the presidency in this country using strong foreign policy as a foundation for their campaign almost since the beginning of our nation. With so many prisoners of war still in foreign countries, what good have these foreign policies been to America and its people. It looks like our foreign policies have backfired on us this time.

THE WAR VETERANS

The Veterans of Foreign Wars have been fighting hard (for all war veterans) since the conclusion of WWII to protect the benefits promised them by the United States Government in Washington. Many of our war veterans are disabled. Yet, the aimless elected officials in Washington who never saw combat duty have been putting themselves first, like in everything else.

The American Legion has also been punching it out with the elected ones in Washington on behalf of the veterans.

The Retired Enlisted Association is constantly working to help the veterans and the military retirees to get a fair shake in their well-earned and deserved benefits.

The Social Security Coalition is continuously fighting to protect the earned social security benefits from being robbed by Congress.

The National Association for Uniformed Services is also battling for the retired military personnel and the widows of retirees. Their effort is to keep the hands of Congress off the promised benefits for these retirees and widows.

It appears that the elected officials in Washington do not want anything permanent with regards to a dependable policy (procedure) for any of the above mentioned groups.

A workable policy for all of the above is the responsibility of the Commander In Chief (the President) of the United States. It is his business to let all those in Washington know that he was elected to protect all of the above. Presently this is not happening. The current policy concerning all of the above is like the dew drop on the tip of the leaf; due to fall any time. Not good. It is clear that there is no one to fight for the people in Washington. What a shame.

AMERICAN TROOPS OVERSEAS

Again, it was very fruitful for Germany and Japan to instigate WWII and then lose the war to the Allied forces. The American taxpayers have been forced to fund the costly operations which ensued after the war. They have paid out billions in support of those countries, with nothing to show for it in return. This has caused the U.S. military leaders to put foreign nations above the security of the United States. This has been a major effort on their part because, with the aimless people in Washington, they have to rob Peter to pay Paul to make ends meet.

The American taxpayers are not funding a military force to guard America. Instead, they are funding military puppets at the beck and call of foreign nations. This fact is difficult for the U.S. military personnel to cope with because of family life disruptions.

Children of military personnel take the brunt of the hardship because of the many changes in schools and family life. The people in Washington responsible for these policies cannot identify with the hardship caused by these policies because they never had to cope with a lifestyle like that of military personnel.

If the current policies regarding troops overseas are to be maintained, overseas governments should be made to pay 85% of the cost to finance our presence there. There should be no more free rides. The officials in Washington appear to be afraid that the foreign nations might not like the United Stated if we discontinue our "babysitting" service and require them to do their own work. I say let them get mad at us. It just might be a change for the better. It's time for Americans to heat up and get mad. It's not against the law for Americans to get angry (yet).

AFTER WWII ENDED

America was a nation of toothy smiles enjoying the glory days at the end of WWII. "Big Mom" was standing tall and was very proud. The dollar was worth $1.00 back then. When America spoke, the world population rose to their feet and listened. The United States Government in Washington stood behind the nation and its people 100%.

The massive productions from the war converted back to civilian needs. Automobile production was in full swing with people waiting for the "Made in America" car they had ordered. Radio and farm implement production was also increased. In the 1950's TV and record players were mass produced for retail markets, again with the products being produced right here in America.

New home construction increased because people wanted better homes. They were happy to see the tin roofs disappear. This new construction created many jobs for Americans and all materials used for construction were manufactured within America.

Gas and oil companies also provided many jobs with Tulsa, Oklahoma billed as the "Oil Capitol of the World". This was America back then. Produced with pride in the U.S.A.

Highway construction was increased and provided many Americans with employment. The farmers were well respected in Washington then, producing a variety of needed products to keep America, as well as some foreign countries, well fed and sound. These farmers hired many unskilled workers. Back then America came first.

Women wanted better ice boxes and rugs for their floors and they wanted them to be made in America.

The United States was on a much better footing then because of its sound economy. Our economy now is nothing more than a drip in the faucet by comparison. Back then people were ashamed to be living on handouts because the economy was so good. Clothing and shoe factories hired many thousands to turn out the American made clothes and footwear.

American schools were turning out much better educated students then. Those students really had to hit the books in order to graduate. There were no free rides like there are now. Church attendance was good back then. Our nation as a whole had much better morals and there was no substitute for purity.

People respected and obeyed the law back then. Lawmen were "king" of the streets and there were only a few jails and prisons. Those that were locked up were treated as prisoners and paid the price for breaking the law. Appeals were rarely heard of. They never wanted to return to the prison for a second time. The old song still sings: "My good gal told me you made your bed in sorrow, now sleep on it like a man". This song should be repeatedly played to all the current inmates in our prisons. Let's not forget the inmates surrendered their privileges when they chose to break the law.

Right after the war ended it was still appropriate to render respect to all women and the young ones rendered respect to their elders. Babies were given all the respect and attention they needed because they were viewed as a gift from heaven. Children were rarely abused back then.

The Congress and Senate were not so costly to the taxpayers then. They understood what shame meant and practiced it. The President was elected as a Statesman and served all the people equally. Our present party system splits our nation in more ways than one. America is now standing on shaky legs with no one really in charge even though there are times when all 537 elected ones are the President, or so they think.

Back then there was little globetrotting from our officials in Washington. America pretty much minded her own business like it should be. The Congress and the Senate have no business in foreign affairs. In fact they have proven they cannot handle their own affairs efficiently.

The Secretaries of State usually conducted their business stateside. They appeared to be for America much more then. It takes little skill to cater to foreigners and to put nation and people second. Today their dealings with foreigners have left them empty handed. This is nothing new because empty hands have been common since the inception of America concerning the Secretaries of State. After WWII ended America and its people came first. We do not see it now. Why?

In the period that followed WWII there weren't many Americans married to foreigners. The foreigners now know how to get a foot hold in America even if they have to marry American men. We have many of them now, with some showing that they left their heart in their homeland. They have parked their butts in America for the real Americans to worry with.

Advertisements for foreign products were virtually unheard of in the United States back then. Plumbing supplies, lawnmowers, and car parts were all manufactured in the USA. Americans were still buying government bonds, too. Bond sales were essential to the effort during WWII. Now the loan sharks have almost put bond buying out of business. The government in Washington without bonds is a weak government at best. Looks like the loan sharks have swallowed the bond operations in Washington.

There were few credit cards back then. The people owned the nation and thriving businesses kept the Americans working. They were able to pay with cash and save a little on the side. This is impossible for most Americans now because they have been turned over to the loan sharks whether they like it or not. Credit cards are easy bucks for big business. The way the nation is now being operated, the beginners cannot save any money. They have no choice but to join the loan sharks. No bank account - no choice.

The parents in the post war era were able to help their children get started in life. No more. The government in Washington now has to come first and to hell with the people.

The older people in those days would never screw up the life of the young ones with drugs and booze, or give them misleading information, or victimize them on a sale. Youngsters then could look up to the older ones for sound advice. Most Americans practiced to tell the truth and stood by it. Church leaders did not use God for excuses or promise blessings for money and food. All of us know that God has no need for a bank and that His garden is fruitful. God gave us all the necessary resources to make it here on earth. If we don't, to some it would appear that He could care less. He shouldn't have to do our work for us on earth. So let's not try to talk Him out of something for nothing. It hasn't happened yet.

The G.I. Bill for veterans was handled in a very efficient manner right after the war. Only a few people were on the payroll, but they were able to handle it. Today there are far too many rubbernecks with their hands in it and it simply isn't necessary. The system used today to provide assistance for the veterans is a very inefficient one. There was a time when disabled veterans were properly cared for. The baby boomers of today could care less about them, especially the boomers that never wore a military uniform.

After the war Memorial Day and Veteran's Day were treated as something special. I don't recall stores having sales on those days. They were days to show respect to veterans for their service to the country and for helping to keep us free. The American flag was never abused and it had better never be, or the abuser would pay the price. The flag was displayed in large numbers in those days. Picnickers usually waited to eat until after the ceremonies were over, voicing that dead veterans do not eat. Most of the churches held services to show their respect and offer prayers to the veterans. The veterans were held in very high esteem by the entire nation.

Over-all education was low in the military ranks through the Korean War effort. The military wanted men who could fight and knew how to shoot. Personnel were assigned as TO&E regardless of their level of education. There were no free rides then. Good fighting and shooting could not be replaced with high levels of education. Through the Korean War, military discipline and leadership were still good. Military missions and traditions received full play. Supplies, discipline, leadership, and weapons won WWII for us. There was no room for back talk.

The sale of military clothing to other than military personnel was not seen until after WWII. The army did not get rich by selling military uniforms and other gear to the civilians. This move did not make the U.S. Army look good in the eyes of the public. Some of the surplus items were bought and worn by bums who never served in the military. They wore them to embarrass the military and our nation. This cheapens the military service. Anyway, today I am hearing that the military is broke.

There was a time when military academies were for men only

and were turning out a good product. The men were sent to the academies to be leaders upon graduation. The graduates were assigned to troop duty and field grade officers were never seen coaching sports. Up to the Korean War, Ike appeared to be the only slip-through.

City engineering appeared to be much better in the post-WWII era. At least there were no water holes seen like we are seeing now. Home basements never flooded because of engineering or construction goofs. Washouts in roads were rarely seen. Bridges were soundly constructed and only a few cracks could be found in new streets and highways.

Drinking water could be found to contain foreign matter on occasion, but the tough and hard working Americans knew it merited no attention. This was no place or time for sissies. It was left up to the women to determine if the food was safe to consume. When God created woman He instilled those qualities in her, not in science. America could never have been built with the scare tactics that come from the scientists today. They are certainly a strange lot.

New cars purchased right after the war were efficiently made. It was almost unheard of to have to return a car to a dealer because the car would not perform properly. Cars that were sold were sold as complete. The spare tire and wheel matched the other four tires and wheels. And cars were affordable then. Most Americans could afford to buy a new car. Cars showed a lot of class in those days.

Farming equipment was well built back then, too. Blacksmiths had little welding to do in those days. Most of his work consisted of sharpening plow points, axes, and other tools. Buildings did not have flat roofs on them. Flat roofs cause too much extra work with regards to repairs and frequent replacement. Back then flat roofs were considered shoddy work.

Highway and street crew bosses worked side by side with the crew in those days to make sure the work was done properly and to insure the crew earned their pay. We could sure use a few bosses like that today.

City workers were not permitted to go to donut shops during working hours. Today they can tell all about the donut shops, like how many flirting women work there. And judging by the reported divorces, some of the flirting went beyond eye rolling. Men do not marry donuts and are not paid by the city to go to donut shops during working hours.

Back in the good old days the priests could be seen dancing with a hoe or a rake at weddings. Women must have told them that they had more to offer than a gardening tool. Hoe and rake dancing are no longer seen today. The priesthood was a much more serious business then.

Before and during WWII the military chaplains made the rounds to the mess halls before first call to show appreciation to the cooks on duty. They did not fall for ear bending tactics. I remember once a soldier complained to a chaplain and the chaplain told the soldier his complaint was not valid because he was the only soldier in the entire regiment with the complaint. The soldier got with the program and became a good soldier. I recall one time we were on maneuvers when rain fell all night long and the water was about ankle deep in our area. It was Sunday morning and the chaplain was making his rounds at the mess halls when he slipped into the kitchen sump hole. Rather than leave to change his clothes and begin late, the chaplain stayed and performed the service on time. The soldiers, always quick to evaluate a situation, said we would all have a good chance of going to heaven because the chaplain prayed for us with greasy lips. No, a good rain in those days couldn't stop a military chaplain. I've seen them use the hood of a jeep for an altar in the field. They have to be hard and strong to survive. They are good people for sure.

In those days there weren't many card and gift shops. Now there are greeting cards for any occasion, even cards for dogs and cats. I once struck up a conversation with a man about greeting cards. I told him that I had the same ones for each occasion: anniversary, wife's birthday, Mother's Day, Christmas, and Easter. He called me a cheap man. Then I told him my reason for it was to prove I am still married to the same wife, and he paused for a moment and agreed. A few years later he confided to me that I was right, and voiced that he should have stayed with his first wife. Sometimes it really pays to think it out.

Burials of the deceased were cheap in the good old days. I wish we could say this for today. They are charging more than a dead person is worth. And they are not ashamed to charge big bucks for a few soft words and a ride in a big fancy car. I remember when the dead were transported by wagon to the cemetery.

The birth of a baby in those days didn't cost much. Usually the neighborhood wives and friends got the job done. The mothers in those days knew more about birthing a baby than a single present day nurse. The doctor was rarely called in for a baby's birth. Many of those same mothers are still around today and are very healthy.

In the period right after WWII and in the 1950's all the stores would close on Sunday and on holidays. You could look at the shops and tell it was Sunday or a holiday. Nowadays it's to hell with ceremony and let's make some bucks instead. I don't think that there is so much money that we could not spend it all Monday - Saturday.

Used to bars were never open on Sunday, or at least they waited until after 1 P.M. to open. The heavy tipplers did not die on Sunday because the bar was not open. Today we have too many drunks in this country. Allow me to point out that during the bootleg liquor days we did not have many alcoholics in this country. During the moonshine days most of the locals knew where the stills were located, but the sheriff never did. The booze was usually sold at night. Then the big men sold the federal and state government on the idea of legalizing booze and making a profit off it. Now we have far too many alcoholics and do not have sufficient treatment facilities for them. Furthermore, while America is now more destitute than she ever was, the big cats continue to fatten their wallets.

The Supreme Court in those days did not meddle in petty affairs. Most Americans abided by the law. With the heavy legal load in our country today we need much younger personnel to get the job done. Some of today's Supreme Court Judges look like old wagons, not able to carry the heavy load. A much younger flesh is needed to remove some of the many bends in the road ahead. Their age limit should be 65, or at least no older than 70. It is time for a change here.

The sale of shampoo was rare in those days and what was sold was supposed to have killed out the dandruff. Well, we still have dandruff today. We also have enough shampoos to open a new river with them. No matter, we will always have the dandruff.

The people who built this country did it by drinking the right amount of water to stay healthy. The soft drinks of today must be outselling the water glasses and pitchers. There are so many kinds of soft drinks on sale and every brand claims to be better than the other. If Americans drank the right amount of water, their visits to the doctor would be reduced by a large number. God made the water for the human body, among other uses. Man made soft drinks to make money.

In the good old days the food menu was a simple one and all the family ate what the mother cooked and put on the table. This is not a common scene today. Television ads on different types of foods and which ones to eat (or not to eat) is getting more ridiculous every day. To hear an American scientist tell it, all foodstuffs must first be approved by government inspectors. What should be inspected is the foods from foreign countries before they are shipped to the U.S. for consumption. Perhaps America should start a school for the scientists to learn how to cook and care for food before they are hired to do their snooping and sniffing. This would put them on the right course for sure.

In the period following WWII there was much more respect for the dead. When someone was called by God the people would stop what they were doing and bow their heads, asking God to take care of his or her soul. Even the stiffnecks bowed their heads then. Now, in too many cases, the dead are ignored and the insurance, if any, gets all the attention. How much insurance did the deceased have, was it good, and who will get it are the chief concerns. The states are not ashamed to grab the earnings of the deceased and this should be against the law. The state did not work for the money. The state agents do not attend funerals because the deceased carry no money when they are buried. Yes, back then there was much more honor upon someone's death. A person could die with dignity and not have to worry about his or her tombstone being stolen. Even at death the money hunters will not go away.

Throughout the WWII era people could leave their key in their car and the car would still be there when they returned. You'd better not try that today. Thieves prowl all night long and sleep very little in the daytime. There are gangs with long hours of operation. At present it appears the thieves outnumber the law enforcement personnel in this country. Often the politicians can be heard claiming they are tough on crime. Those who wear eyeglasses should remove them so that they might see the real truth. Crime is still rapidly growing in this country. Criminals know hot air when they hear it, and they've had plenty to listen to lately.

The personal appearance of Americans was pretty clean cut until the 1960's. This was when the jet gang arrived in Washington. Many barbershops have since gone out of business. The clothing stores are doing quite well, selling rags instead of nice clothes. The women fell for the new styles and were, and still are, seen in public showing more skin than cloth. The items made of practically nothing cost more simply because they are the new style. That is called traveling light in public. Some of the people in show business are trying to cover themselves a little by using a broken guitar string.

At present not many of the traditional dressers are a problem to others or in the nation. Since the inception of America, the grandmas have been looking out the corner of their eye in disapproval of the fashions preferred by the younger generation. To date they have not whipped it. Instead, the new styles are being advertised on TV and in newspapers. It would seem that improvement in the matter of appearance is not to be seen in the near future. Even young boys dress like walking bags, thinking they are number one in their appearance. They sure don't know good taste when it comes to dressing themselves.

I don't think that I am that out of date on the personal appearance matter or that I am practicing to be an old snoop. It's just a good thing that God has not ordered his Mother Mary to earth to take a look at how the Americans dress. If she hit the ground in the summer months she would be way overdressed compared to the light travelers in America. Her feedback would be: No way could your powerful eyes absorb it all. My eyes are overfilled with bare skin. I am ready to come home.

Americans were basically treated equally throughout the Vietnam War era. President Lyndon B. Johnson was a good ole country boy and did pretty much what he felt he had to do. Then the Republicans came into office and made it seem as though the Democrats were no good and neither were you if you didn't vote the Republican ticket. Since then both parties have been making the same noise, each claiming the other are not up to par. I think if you are no good because you belong to the wrong party, you should be excused from taxes while the opposing party is in office. If this were so the present complaining wouldn't hold up for very long. Neither party could care less where the money comes from as long as it comes to Washington for them to use. The Democrats should have been excused from paying taxes for twelve years and now the Republican should be excused for at least the next four years. This would bring it true to light that the present mouthings are horsestuff.

In the 1980's America had to deal with the Iran-Contra scandal. The scandal cost the Americans dearly just to listen to a lot of noise. This was the first time since the conclusion of WWII that the United States could have made a little money. Instead, the taxpayers continue to carry the financial burden. The Democrats played dumb, claiming they knew nothing about it. Yet, they made most of the noise in the hearings.

Neither party is heard from when it comes to an answer for balancing the budget. That's where all the noise should be coming from, asking "What is the delay?". That bull and cow stuff cheapens America throughout the entire world. The President should have told them and the nation that other countries are doing it and I am standing behind my men and nation 100%. Instead he beat it to California to escape the political heat in Washington. The special prosecutor should have been investigating those who have wasted a ton of U.S. dollars on foreign countries with nothing to show for it. As it turns out, it has cost the American taxpayers over 30 million dollars to see which party could make the most noise concerning the Iran-Contra scandal.

The 1980's also gave us the big S&L blunder to cope with. Both parties knew of the problem before the election of 1988. This is one time in recent events that both parties played the same old game: you scratch my back and I'll scratch yours. They made it look like not one elected official in Washington was guilty. And as usual, the burden of repayment was shifted to the taxpayer. Now in the 90's we have Whitegate going on. I suggest we lay it all on the table from A to Z and let the chips fall where they may. Include the man who signed the deregulation without supervision bill that allowed for easy grabbing of the money by hungry hands. Let's not forget Watergate, when the President got an early ride to California because he did not want to face the facts concerning the matter. Truth always fits better than a lie.

The elected officials in Washington like to meddle in how the foreign nations should have their countries function and how they should vote the American way. I say let's clean out the disorganized mob and start giving the American people more on the lines of what they deserve.

We have sent troops to Somalia and to Bosnia to help settle their government's differences and to feed the hungry. All the while we have Americans living without safety in the cities and going hungry in the streets. All of our elected officials need to look inland, not abroad. Most of what's happening abroad is none of our business in the first place. America is now saturated with crime, unsafe practices, and fraud in areas like the foodstamp program. In order to clean this mess up, all Americans will have to don their work clothes for at least the next 5 years.

When the floods came to the midwest not all the people in the area helped where they could. They are the ones who are doing all the crying about how hard it is to live in America. The National Guard should never be ordered to do what civilians can do for themselves. The city mayors and state governors are overdue to get their feet wet when it comes to a plan of action in the flood areas.

COST OF MILITARY HARDWARE

The cost of military hardware is not easy on the taxpayers pocket book. The present costs are outrageously high and, again, the taxpayers are being taken. There is no way under the current procedures that the United States could fight WWII with the same success it did the first time around. Corporate greed has taken over the respect for the nation and its people. It is not too late to investigate over charging for products by these companies. The President did initiate an investigation during WWII and the violators were caught flat footed. All charges above normal were returned to the government.

The high prices for military hardware began in the 1980's. Now it has been proven that a president in a wheelchair who wants to protect the nation and its people is a much better president than a fast talking president on his horse. It is time, and long overdue, to stop this injustice on the taxpayers.

It would be very interesting if the hardware makers were made to provide maintenance personnel to maintain the equipment they sell to the government. They would quickly learn that at times they have been making junk out of junk for our military forces. If it weren't for this mediocre hardware, surely the dead-line rate of military equipment would be much lower than what it has been and is now. Motor pools are now showing a large number of retriever vehicles ready for constant towing. It is not unusual to see a retriever towing a retriever. Parts departments and warehouses are larger than ever.

Yes, the present costs for military hardware are much too high and should not be permitted continue. Let's stop treating the hardware manufacturers as friends. Instead we should treat them as the enemy to the taxpayers they are.

MILITARY RETIREES

Military retirees have lost most of their dental benefits and all other benefits are due to fall at any time. These benefits were earned by the retirees. In combat they ducked bullets and shrapnel. Now they are ducking the political bull and cow pancakes. Let's face it. If we had no veterans we wouldn't have a United States. It was beneficial for Germany and Japan to initiate WWII and then lose it. Both countries are rolling in American Foreign aid, with ample financing to take care of their veterans and retirees.

Military retirees have paid a high price for what few benefits they have. Yet, the residents in our prison system receive better medical care than that earned by our military retirees. Military retirees earned their benefits by fighting for the United States of America, while the prisoners are granted theirs for killing and robbing good Americans.

I never gave any thought to the fact that if I, as a military retiree, were to continue to receive my once promised benefits that I would have to go to prison or overseas to receive them. This is shameful to the United States of America and to all good Americans. It certainly proves that the state and federal governments have lost their direction in the matter of military retiree benefits.

We never hear of the 537 elected officials in Washington losing any of their benefits. The government is not standing by the military retirees with its promises. Instead, the promises have turned out to be a big lie. Military retirees are treated like stray dogs. Every once in a while the retirees are tossed a bone to bait them along. The current predicament is a culmination of events over the last 12 years. The American working class has not caused the situation. All of us know who owns the dirty hands. They are the ones who want the retiree medical benefits monies to fall into the pockets of civilians.

If all the personnel who died in wars for the United States could see what they died for, they would be thoroughly disappointed with what has become of the United States Government in Washington. They all died bravely for America and its people so the children and nation would have a sound future ahead of them. It is difficult to see this ideal now.

It would be insightful for the elected officials in Washington and other critics to pay a visit to the burial sites of military retirees and veterans. One can almost hear the grass groan around their graves. And for those resting at the bottom of the ocean, the sea waters always render full respect. They are the true heroes. Those retirees and veterans still alive are the living statues of freedom and our way of life.

Let's stop giving the old horse a whipping for winning the race on the battlefields for the United States of America. That is a poor way of saying "thank you, men, for keeping us free". Those who fought for the United States of America deserve a fair deal.

WISHFUL THINKING

Those Americans who think that the rich Republicans will give them a little something will have to ask God for an extension on this earth because they will not see it in one lifetime. Most of the businesses that moved to Mexico and overseas are owned by the Republicans. Their loyal American workers were left behind like dogs. This proves that Republicans place money first and people as second, or not at all. But to hear the Republicans tell it, there is not one bad Republican in business in America.

Our nation and its people have been getting plenty of statistics from both parties in Washington. If we, as Americans, paid our bills with statistics we would all be in jail.

Our last president recommended the Congress and Senate for pay raises and then bitched like hell when they refused to work with him. He tried to be "Mr. Nice Guy" with the taxpayer's money, but was fooled by the recalcitrants. Again, the Vice President cooled it and the officials got away with it.

Both parties like to tell how great things are in this country. To date neither party has furnished a list of banks that are bankrupt, loan companies that went under, or the number of businesses that have closed shop because of one sided foreign trade. It appears that there are not enough good ones left in Washington to fight for America and people.

Word has it that both parties knew about the Savings & Loan blunder before the 1988 presidential election. They chose to keep quiet rather than inform the American public. The man responsible for the deregulation without supervision got away scott free. Only a few scapegoats got roped and pulled into the stockades. The big boys in this country can do no wrong and are never required to follow the rules like the rest of us do. Our officials in

Washington are expected to set an example for us all to follow. We don't see it now.

The Congress and Senate have about 37,000 employees (piddlers) on their payroll. This is more than two army divisions. Yet, the Congress is still talking about more cuts in the military because the military, in their opinion, is too fat. The Congress and Senate are approximately the size of one army battalion. If our military used 37,000 troops to support one battalion it would be viewed as completely ludicrous. Now, who is the one that is really too fat?

The Congress and Senate never include themselves into the many sacrifices others must make. They continue to live on easy street without consideration for others. Their 37,000 piddlers are of no value to our national defense. They are living much better than the Americans that must work so hard to make the paychecks available to the officials.

If all Americans were put into groups of 535 people, there would not be enough Americans left to provide each group with 37,000 people to serve them. Two clerks per Congressman and Senator are more than enough. Please show us how much each is paid every month.

BIG GOVERNMENT

In the 1950's the Republican administration increased the number of Federal Civil Service employees up into the millions. We now have no way of shrinking this group of employees without a big fight. These employees are merely paperwork creators.

In regards to the single woman, lightening might strike and she may find a husband. The "piddlers" simply get to retire with two retirement checks in their later years. One check comes from the government retirement system and one from Social Security. This is a very easy way to have their toast buttered on both sides. They have fought no wars and performed no field duty. They should retire solely on Social Security checks like the rest of the working class must do in the civilian sector. Not having to pay them fat retirement checks would save millions of dollars for the taxpayers.

Let us not forget there was no need for dumpsters on military installations until the Federal Civil Service arrived. Now we have reports, reports, and more reports for all Americans and for businesses.

We should begin in Washington to clean up the Federal Civil Service personnel. The military had simple and very efficient operations until the "Feds" arrived. Military personnel have to get the operations going before the civilians arrive in the mornings, take their places during lunch hour, and fill their places when the civilians depart for home.

Civilians should be removed from assignments in military hospitals. This would give the hospitals the needed uplift if they were routed out. Military hospitals are not an eight-hour operation. The emergency rooms have become less than a joke, with both military and civilian women in various stages of pregnancy on the job.

At the present time no one seems to know how to explain the space available system of care to the military retirees. About two years ago I counted 40 beds in a military hospital, with only eight beds being used by patients. The following Friday two of those patients were released to go home for the weekend. The military doctors have a very tough task to cope with, trying to operate the hospitals under the present setup. There is no way the military hospitals could take in wounded from the battlefield under the current procedures. If we put military personnel in the places of civilians, operations would noticeably improve. It would also be gainful to the American taxpayers to utilize military personnel.

FOREIGN AID

In order to get better use from the monies, control of foreign aid needs to be taken from the hands of the Congress and the Secretary of State and placed under the control of the U.S. Treasurer and the Vice President. Many foreign nations are our friends only as long as the money lasts. Billions of dollars have been wasted on foreign countries since the end of WWII, with nothing in return to show for it. Word has it in the mountain country that the Germans and the Japanese no longer want to drink socially with the Americans. Now they expect to be paid for it.

For over forty years, the Secretaries of State have been driving their ducks to a very poor market. To allow this to continue is completely absurd. Foreign money should be voted on by the American public every time we vote for a president. The money belongs to the American taxpayer, not the Secretary of State. To hell with the foreign countries for a change. Let's use the money right here in America to create jobs and a future for our people.

It really paid for Germany and Japan to start WWII and then lose it. They have been rolling in American foreign aid ever since. Americans are being put out of a job while the officials in Washington continue to put the foreigners needs first, and to hell with our own nation and its people.

Wherever we look in America there is not enough money to pay the bills. For example, the schools had to extend their Christmas vacation because there was not enough money to pay the utility bill. And this is not the only place where the bill(s) cannot be paid. The State of Colorado is not alone in the money shortage. The foreign aid money handlers need to look past Washington D.C. to really see what's going on in this nation.

After WWII ended General George Patton remained in Europe for awhile. He sent word to Marshall that unless we (the United States) acted fast, the communists would take over Germany and perhaps some other European countries. Shortly after that, Patton was killed in an auto accident and was buried with other soldiers from WWII in a cemetery in Europe. Marshall took credit for the plans made to keep European countries free. The United States government started the so-called George Marshall Plan to rebuild Germany and Japan. Only Marshall was no Patton when it came to telling it straight.

The main reason for the Marshall Plan was to protect the Germans from starvation and deaths by freezing in the winter of 1945. A lot of wood cutting was done by the German people and the American soldiers stationed there. Japan received very much the same kind of support from the United States. Both countries must have been extremely cold and hungry, because the foreign aid is still being continued for them nearly fifty years later. That is some pretty big stomachs and slow warming bodies.

What is ironic is that both countries seem to be more financially established than the United States currently is. It is time to stop the foreign aid and let Germany and Japan fend for themselves. The money saved could certainly be put to much better use right here in America.

The government in Washington likes to make it look like America can do everything to help other countries, even if we have to go broke to prove it. The American economy has been gutted to the bone in an effort to please the foreign countries and we can no longer afford to be Mom and Dad for the world. America (Big Mom) is starving for a policy to sustain herself. The time is upon us to put America first.

George Marshall rode the gravy train in Washington. We made him a big hero by winning WWII. We put an end to the WAR conflagration. Now the military personnel are being eliminated from service because of lack of money to pay them. Yet, the money for foreign aid continues to roll out in the billions. When our young men joined the military service they were told they had a 20 year career if they wanted it. This is no longer true. Many will get their walking papers long before they can complete 20 years of service. This boils down to putting the foreigners above the American people when it comes to money.

The only reason we still have a United States of America is because of the diligent efforts of our military forces. Where is the justice for the Americans in all of this? It is continually proven that the foreigners come first.

The officials who continue to shame the Americans are not on the same footing as those people that do not live in Washington D.C. Americans strive for equal opportunity among her own people, and they surely deserve equal opportunity with regards to foreigners. America is being put to shame in this respect.

Since the conclusion of WWII foreign countries showed us they have many people with long arms and big hands to catch the American dollars. Yet, they give nothing in return for all our efforts. Their arms must be made of tempered steel because they have never tire of reaching for the Yankee dollar. When are the officials in Washington going to stick up for the American people and our nation? We, as citizens, are tired of waiting.

We have spent some big bucks to train our military personnel, and now it looks like it was a big joke. Recruiting our military personnel was not free either. The officials in Washington are displaying a lack of respect for the hard earned tax dollars used to finance these operations. During all this "hoedown" the American people have been mere puppets.

And what about the military personnel that were given their walking papers? In the event of an emergency, will they want to fight for their country and government; the same government that said they weren't needed?

The time is now for the 537 elected officials in Washington to get their heads screwed on straight and put America and her people back on the front burner where they belong. It has been said many times not to give a beggar a horse for nothing in return. The beggar will ride away laughing and then return to ask, "Who will furnish feed and care for my horse?" This is pretty much the way foreign aid has been working for the United States for over forty years. This is a long time for hard working Americans to be compelled to sleep with a corpse. Enough is enough.

MEDDLING IN FOREIGN AFFAIRS

With so much to be accomplished at home, Americans have no time to be meddling overseas. The United States has been involved in so many foreign matters that we, as Americans, have lost favor with the people overseas that we are trying to help.

If the Secretaries of State continue to spend so much time abroad, they will need a refresher course in English. Their oily conversations have produced few results, if any. If foreign countries want our help, let them come to America to seek it.

For many years the Secretaries of State have been greasing the palms of foreign dignitaries. The Secretaries should be asking where the U.S. dollars could best be spent in America. Thus far, not one word has been said. If the State Department personnel were paid on their accomplishments there would be plenty of growling guts in that department. They certainly need to show more respect for the American working class and their tax money.

This nation has had many men that ran for president whose platform was based on strong foreign policy. America is overdue for a strong policy for the United States. There cannot be two suns in the sky in Washington, D.C.

THE TAKE DOWN OF THE BERLIN WALL

The Berlin Wall is gone, but the problems in Europe remain. The German people are now squabbling over property and other areas, one claiming to own the property while the other claims the same. This should have been expected.

Many of the older Germans from the WWII era have since passed away. The German baby boomers are now indulging in a tug of war, both sides trying to prove that they are right. It is costing the German Government dearly to resettle their country.

American foreign aid was one idea to help the Germans with the money problems.

I do not know if the Americans complied with the foreign aid request, but I do know that Russia did not leave there on a friendly note. They actually had to be paid to leave what was once East Germany. The amount was estimated at $5 billion. This continues to prove the Russians will not do anything for nothing. The Russian Army that was pulled out of what was once East Germany was redesignated from army to the navy. The Russians claim to be a peaceful country now. We shall see.

The President of the U. S., at the time of the Russian departure from Berlin, stated that it was his tough policy towards the Russians that ran them out of East Germany. Since the Russians had to be paid to leave, it is apparent that the President's tough Hollywood talk didn't frighten the Russians very much. Nor were they so frightened by the pregnant female American soldiers that they beat it back to Russia.

Furthermore, since the fall of the Berlin Wall the United States has been busy destroying large numbers of weapons, all the while trying to get the Russkies to do the same. Thus far, the Russians have not made it known where they have destroyed one army rifle.

The American working class and other taxpayers paid big bucks for the hardware during the era of the Berlin Wall, only to see this hardware go up in smoke. Our foreign policies are such that the Americans can, in no way, gain forward momentum in any of them. The Berlin Wall should have been shot down while it was being constructed, not so many years later. This has proven to be another wishful thinking venture.

WASHINGTON PARTIES

Information has it that it takes approximately 96 chow hustlers to carry off a White House party. That number is equal to one WWII battery of officers and enlisted men in a 155mm howitzer battery. Still, the military's top command must continue to reduce its forces to meet the demands placed upon them by Congress, the Senate, and the President himself.

The chow hustlers will have to be very accurate while throwing dishes at the enemy to inflict the same type of damage to the enemy as the 155mm howitzer battery. Our elected officials sure enjoy living on Easy Street.

CONGRESSIONAL PAY RAISES

Congress once voted themselves a pay raise in the amount of $23,000 per year. For what? All it did was get this nation deeper in debt. Let's face it. If all Americans made $23,000 per year we would be a nation of toothy smiles. We certainly pay our Congress a lot of money for them to screw up the national debt, budget, and country. How would they like to have it done to them the way are doing it to us? This proves that they put themselves above the people and law of this nation. This is totally wrong on the part of the members of Congress.

EQUAL OPPORTUNITY

The best way to unite this country is make the people (all Americans) pay their fair share of taxes, have the 537 elected officials pay their own way like all other Americans must, and to require Congress to obey the laws they pass. When these three areas of concern are rectified, we will truly be looking at equal opportunity. Those who will not comply with them are not true Americans.

Both political parties have formed a gap between the children, senior citizens, working class and the Congress, Senate, and the rich. For many of the underdogs, about the only time they get to ride in a long, fancy car is from the funeral home to the cemetery. At that point it is too late for them to enjoy the ride.

Nowadays, the babies in America have a very bleak future ahead of them, with no one to look up to at the top of our government.

SOCIAL SECURITY

Our Congress and Senate have been doing a superb job of keeping the social security system screwed up. Every time the working class of America builds up the monies in social security the officials in Washington destroy their efforts by removing the funding from social security without so much as a word.

The funds in our social security system should be earning interest for the people and nation. This can't be happening now, with so much shuffling of the funding taking place. The people of America are tired of the current practices.

The souls of those in Washington must be upside down for them to treat the social security efforts like they have been handling them. Is this their best? I think not. At the present time I think only some of their worst is showing.

The elected people are now robbing the MEDICARE Funds too. In both, a stop to both is a must.

COALITIONS

I once saw a list of 26 coalitions, and there are more of them to fight the Congress and the Senate off. All of the elected officials have been chosen to be custodians of the monies of our nation. Instead of being responsible and dependable, our congressmen have proven they cannot be trusted in the matter of our nation's funds. The interest on the national debt is now $1 billion per day and growing.

Now, the Congress just finished voting on balancing the budget. Enough of them voted "yes" on NAFTA, making matters worse for the American working class, those looking for a job, and for the students graduating this year.

Will you be working in the unemployment offices of your home towns to learn the job market? Those of you that voted "yes" on NAFTA should not let this opportunity go by. There is a huge surprise awaiting you.

SNOOPING ON OTHERS

Republicans enjoy exposing the past of others. As of yet, they have not told us that the women they married were all virgins, nor that the men they married were all saints. Real Americans could care less about their bull and cow stuff. Instead, Americans want jobs and a sound future for themselves, their children and their nation.

The news media like to jump on the political sex scandals while they themselves are not all saints and virgins. Both the Republicans and the media folks must think that the American public is totally stupid.

Few Republican and media people are seen lighting candles in the churches on Sunday. Don't do as we do, but do as we say seems to be the curve here.

THE CONGRESS AND THE SENATE

Our elected officials in Washington, D.C. are supposed to set an example for us all, not unlike our fathers and mothers. They are being lousy mothers and fathers when they fill their bellies at the dinner table and leave the scraps to the others. They have the Internal Revenue Service to appropriate the monies they need in Washington and the taxpayers get to keep what little money is left. This gives them a free ticket all the way to sustain themselves and to hell with all others.

The officials in Washington are a cold hearted stock for sure. The money appropriated to them is sometimes not all spent. Instead of turning the excess funds back in to the government, they often keep the overage for themselves. This is not their money to keep. It belongs to the American people. In a sound business operation this is called theft.

If all Americans behaved like our elected officials there is no way America could survive. If all Americans behaved in such an aimless manner there would be no America. To our Congress and Senate: Please join us and become part of those who care for the nation and about its people.

CONGRESSIONAL TERM LIMITS

Legislation is needed now to limit the time spent in Washington by our Congressmen and Senators. We should allow them to spend only 4 months in Washington per year. They have proven to all that they can inflict enough damage to this nation and its people in 4 months. If their time in Washington cannot be limited, then put them on an allowance pay schedule with base pay, rations, quarters and no more. This type of compensation will require them to have to pay their own way like all other Americans must do. Let them rough it with the rest of us for a change. These officials should be limited to a lifetime service of 12 years, with a modest retirement compensation for their services.

Legislation is also needed to cover absent officials. When they miss one day of their work, then they will lose one day of their pay. No more free rides. If the American working class did what the officials did there would be no payday for them. The officials' motto should be: We shall lead by example in all operations from now on. Just watch us.

It is an honor for good Americans to be honest.

BOTH PARTIES (DUPLICATE NAME)

There never was and never will be such a thing as a good Republican or a good Democrat unless one is a good American first. Good Americans always put the United States of America and its people first in all aspects. Both parties have been promising it will be done in the next hitch, but the time for keeping the promise never seems to come. The people of this nation are tired of looking for a better tomorrow. Being a puppet in this country is not easy. Let us recapture the America of old.

Our nation and its people deserve more than they are getting now. Big Mom (the United States) is now showing very tired hands and arms trying to keep her underwear on. The people long for dependability from Washington officials. America is like a company and must be operated like one, with proper accounting of funds and a five year plan for the future so the people will know what's in store for them.

This is where the high and college students and the unemployed come in. They should all be heard from. This is a must. Right now there is no plan of any kind for their future. Our elected ones seem to put the foreign countries first and the Americans second, or not at all.

The American working class now have to sit very carefully due to the shafting they are getting from Washington. If the officials would join the working class they would quickly learn that the present system cannot be tolerated any longer. The problems in Washington (the Congress and the Senate) are why many Americans will not vote. You don't have to look around. Those of you who fit the bill know who you are.

To date neither the Republicans nor the Democrats have told us why the United States Marines were killed in the Middle East. Nothing has been said about the large number of foreclosures in this country. And what about the number of jobs that have gone from 40 hours a week to less than 40 hours a week? We never hear anything said about the workers who have lost their insurance coverage from their employer in the last few years. Another silent subject is the unemployment rate, as well as the rise in prices for food and other goods.

It cost more today to buy a bicycle than it used to cost for a good used car. Things are not so great as the officials in Washington think when looked at through the eyes of the working class.

And remember, the officials in Washington never smell sweaty on their jobs.

BALANCING THE BUDGET

The elected ones in Washington, D.C. seem to think there is no need to balance the budget of our nation. Well, not all the people in America make a living like the officials in Washington do. The officials that voted not to balance the budget should be voted out of office as soon as possible.

Our nation can no longer withstand the kind of treatment it is currently receiving from our officials. To begin with the officials should have to take a cut in pay. They are the ones that created the budget problems. In Washington we have people counting owls in the dark that consistently come up with correct counts. Others can count the swift moving perch while they swim in the water and a few others can pick out the quail in the weeds. Yet these same people are unable to count our tax dollars in the light of day. We have snail counters and dove counters whose numbers must be correct in order for them to remain on the payroll. In all these counters we still have no one to properly count our tax dollars.

Our nations symbol, the bald eagle, is always properly counted. The counts of other birds and why they can fly such a long distance with only a single drink of water must be correct. Why is it that our tax dollars are not properly counted?

The bees have been counted so much they are beginning to lose the sting in their tails. The ants have been counted, too. The count on the wild horses seems to be correct. The fox and coyote counts are all right, along with the counts of all the fish in the oceans.

There appears to be no problems with the number of people that fall in love, or the number of people that snore. All out efforts have been made to accurately count the number of soldiers that urinate before they attack the enemy.

The count of the campaign funds is up to date. If this select area of our tax dollars can be accounted for it seems like the rest could get an accurate count as well.

COMPLETING PROJECTS ON TIME

Current practices indicate the government in Washington D.C. is not concerned with completing projects on time. For example, the government has worked for many years on pollution, showing little improvement on its cleanup. Along with pollution, there are many other projects being nursed along just to keep the jobs that support them. Most of these projects show very little results.

Instead of completing projects, the government adds fear to the people. If present policy is permitted to continue, all of us should be prepared to pay $5 per belch, and $10 each time the backside vapor is released. The piddlers in Washington have failed us; they have shown the need for more capable people to do the job.

When projects are not completed on time, they usually cost the taxpayers extra money. Instead of paying the contractors extra money for not completing a job on time, why not fine them for not being finished by the date agreed on. We should also hit the government supervisors in the pocket for catering to these contractors. Contractors' tricks for more money have been very costly to the taxpayers. These manipulations cannot be permitted to continue.

From now on let's protect the taxpayers, not the contractors. The contractors have had all the fun they are going to have. American taxpayers deserve better.

GOVERNMENT INSPECTORS, SNOOPS, AND SNIFFERS

Government personnel are snooping on farmers, ranchers, chickens and their eggs. They are inspecting cows, hogs, and fish. They count the eagles, the owls and the quail. They try to determine why people fall in love, what causes men to snore, and why whales crave the sand on the beaches. They inspect the flies on fruit trees, the milk to determine why it is sometimes unsafe for people, and the water to insure it is safe to drink. They instill fright among the people where cancer is concerned. They test the soil if it has a funny odor, test and approve new drugs, and anything else that might seem important. The problem is they are in no hurry to complete their testing and inspecting.

With so many undetermined results they have the American people so frightened that they are afraid to take a deep breath. If these inspectors are permitted to continue with the present scare tactics (fanned by the media) we all better prepare to pay $5.00 per belch and $10.00 every time we release the back side vapor.

Soon this country will have more inspectors than it has farmers to inspect. What a shame that it is against the law to eat government inspectors.

Small businesses have been forced to close up shop because of big businesses. The small farmer is now a has-been as well. Government tries to tell us why some children are unable to learn certain subjects, like they can see into a child's skull. This is big government just giving us more scary talk to cope with. When we get rid of about 85% of them the country will be on a much more efficient course.

Changes are long overdue here. Taxpayers should not be made to fund the government's meddling and high living. The time has come to tell the sniffers and snoopers good bye.

AMERICAN WOMEN

American women are the best in the world and are unbeatable in all aspects. They have to work whether they want to or not. They work to support their family, the government in Washington, and the foreign countries. It is the women who provide the military personnel that fight the wars for foreign nations. Many times their sons do not come back alive, while other sons return with permanent combat wounds. Some of their sons are left behind, as prisoners of war, to rot away in some enemy country. The American women also give us the sons and daughters better known as the American working class; the class that keeps America afloat.

American women have to face many challenges to rear their children in today's society. With all the "bait" in the cities and towns (like drugs, booze, game machines) it is difficult at best to raise your children right. Some women have to take their children to and from school because of child molesters who were released from prison because they appeared to be a "nice" guy. A lot of women themselves have been molested but did not report it for fear of being laughed at in the courtroom.

Many women are lied to by the men when they are asked to marry them. Many are promised eternal happiness only to be abandoned. Runaway fathers can not provide eternal happiness.

Most women have to leave everything familiar when they marry and go to where the husband's career takes them. Even when it is clear across the United States, the women do not complain. Not many American women marry foreigners. They are the first to say that only half-assed Americans will marry a foreigner.

American women enjoy beautiful flowers and render them full care. The good American women always practice good manners. The watchful ones rarely get into trouble because they know what the limits are and how to avoid it.

Through most divorces in America it is usually the women and the children who have to face the facts of hardship. Through the suffering the women still stand by their child(ren) to the end.

Women are very active in the church. It is the women who make the churches look nice, even pretty, during Christmas and Easter, among other important church events. When the women attend church services they pay attention to what is being said up in front. Their mind is not cluttered with begging forgiveness for the past week's mischief. It's a good thing they are not permitted to bring hatchets with them to the services. A few men's heads might be split in order to dig out what they are thinking. Yes, women pay much more attention in the church than do the men. The men usually give the impression they are more concerned with who will look after them when it's all over for them on earth.

Women offer help to the needy ones when possible. They are much more considerate than men. Many times a woman will buy what she doesn't need because it might help the working ones put food on their table. I see this at our house often.

Women pretty much mind their own business and do not cut down those who get out of line a little. She will merely point out that what others do is their business. Men often blame women for idle gossip when in fact men gossip more than women. The men tend to get away with it because they call it "judging". Women have a lot of faith in mother nature and are able to smooth things over when things are going rough.

American women know how to approach their husband without making him blow his top when the children need a little extra help. Many women have to rough it alone for two or more years when her military husband is assigned overseas to babysit the foreigners. While he is away the mother has to be everything, both mother and father, nurse, etc. She continues to function on the home front the best she can without her husband's help.

When the time comes to move her household, the American woman assumes the position of First Sergeant and Commander. As First Sergeant she assigns duties to the children and takes on the role of Commander to make sure the assigned tasks have been properly completed. When the move to overseas is completed the woman has to start anew because the foreign country's rule and government are not the same as in America. American women maintain a full payload of patience to remain strong and diligent.

Non-military women do not have it easy either. There are many husbands who are salesmen, firemen, guardsmen, etc. Men who are often absent for long periods of time. These non-military women have the same responsibilities to maintain.

American women have a never ending list of home chores to do, regardless of their age. Homemakers walk farther in their lifetime than do most soldiers. They have to make a plan for the month, each month of the year, to keep the home and family going, including many changes in their own plans.

The American mother is the one that has to deal with teenage pregnancy and at times does not receive the required support from the parents of the young man responsible for the pregnancy. The young man that fathered the child should not be allowed to get out of his responsibilities.

American women do not sleep much when their own child is born. However, they do not cave in to the stress. Instead they crave another child to have another challenge in life.

American women are more apt to give free advice. They do a superb job as nurses, secretaries, bookkeepers, and stenographers. They are adept at handling air traffic, acting as stewardess, and selling the flight tickets in airports.

Women are wonderful cashiers at food stores because they have a genuine concern and understanding for the mother on her way home from work needing to cook the family meal when she gets home. Men cashiers cannot compete with them on the same level. Women also do an outstanding job in the retail clothing stores selling the products.

American women are at their best during the Christmas season, along with Thanksgiving and Easter, preparing feasts and keeping the children perked up.

I think that when God created man that he should have seen to it that every man would have to bear one child and raise it in his lifetime. If this were the case, we would not have as many runaway and careless fathers in America and our prison population would be a much small number. There would also be fewer fathers abusing their children. (Please do not misunderstand this as pointing a critical finger at God.)

You will never hear of woman going to hell. She has already lived her hell right here on earth.

AMERICAN MOTHERS

American mothers should not have to work outside the home unless they choose to, but many mothers have no choice in the matter if their family's needs are to be met. Many mothers are forced to work nights and weekends just to make ends meet. This situation separates families and in some cases is the root of the wrongdoing of the children. Our American mothers deserve better than this.

With an ever-growing money hunger (greed) in Washington, mothers in America really have to watch their backs in an effort to have enough resources to buy food for their children. Our mothers hate to see the taxpayers money go overseas when there are so many needy right here in our own country. The pocket pickers in Washington are showing our mothers no mercy.

THE GRANDMOTHERS

Not many grandmothers are enjoying their golden years. Many grandmothers are continuing to work, either for themselves or they take care of their grandchildren to help their children make ends meet. They have no need for a fingernail file. Their nails are kept short by searching their purses for coins to find enough money to pay for groceries. Many grandmothers can be seen walking to and from their shopping, for lack of any other transportation. Our grandmothers deserve a better standard of living.

Grandfather is not excused from helping the needy ones in the family either. I know because I am a grandfather and I take the time to help those in my family.

It appears that not all grandparents in America will enjoy their golden years until a halt is brought to the pocket picking by those in Washington. They make it very difficult to be an old person in America today. The foreigners come first in Washington, with the elderly coming in second or not at all. The elderly have certainly earned a better status than this.

Because of their financial state many of the elderly are forced to stay near their homes. It is a shame that the word "vacation" is rarely heard in their conversations. Often times they are unable to see their children that live out of their area because the grandparents cannot afford to travel and neither can their children.

Government officials need to take a closer look at this situation to ascertain what is truly going on in this nation. If the founding fathers of America could see what has been done to this nation by the wheelers and dealers in our top government, they would be physically ill. The only way to stop this injustice is for the American people to remove the current officials and replace them with new officials who will put America and its people first, like it used to be.

AMERICAN SINGLE WOMEN

Single women in America should also be able to say "no" to employment, unless they so choose to work. Much time is needed to prepare themselves for marriage and future motherhood. In most cases, the single woman does not have the luxury of extra time. These women are forced to go to work (if they can find a job) or they go hungry because their parents can, or will, no longer provide for them. This is shame and should be remedied by those responsible.

BABIES BORN IN AMERICA

If all the babies born in the United States opened their eyes with the ability to see and read the $17,000 debt they each would owe the government, their voices could be heard throughout the nation: "Back! Back! Put us back! We want no part of this!"

The mothers in our country really have to watch their flanks in order to have enough to eat. Officials in Washington are showing them no mercy.

The Republicans would have us believe they are very conservative. Yet, just over twelve years ago Americans owed only $4000 each to the government. There is no market for their full payload of horse droppings.

Both parties in Washington are on the big spender's spree. This can only happen when there is no one really in charge at the top of our government. The children of our nation deserve better than this.

AMERICAN MERCHANTS, "SALES", AND SET PRICES

We, as consumers, have to pay for the advertising of American merchants by paying higher prices for goods in order to cover the cost of media ads. This is not fair and its time for this practice to stop. Why not have businesses use specific days, like a Saturday or Wednesday, to have their "specials" and discontinue the use of the media to spread the word? This could bring prices down by a large percent. If the merchants want to continue to use the current methods of advertising, let them use personal funds to pay for it, not the inflated profits of goods that are sold.

Small businesses are continuing to fight to keep their heads above water. America is supposed to be a nation of equal opportunity, but it is not. If set prices were used these small businesses would have a better chance competing with the larger merchants. As it stands now, the big dogs are chewing up the pups.

If this suggestion was put into play, there would be more resources for mothers to provide for their families. It would also reduce the number of food stamps that now have to be used by the not so fortunate. We have nothing to lose here. It's time to stop beating up on the consumers.

American merchants are not bashful when it comes to "sales". Not long ago I saw an ad in the newspaper for mechanical tools. The sale was for Mother's Day. All of us know very well that when God created babies he did not put them together with screws and bolts. Mothers do not need a mechanical tool set to keep a baby tightened up. Fast operating merchants will try anything to make a fast buck.

Three areas gave Jesus his biggest problems when he was on earth. One area was the merchants who displayed their goods for sale on the altar in His temple. Another was the tax collectors that hounded Him for money. The third was the merchants who refused to give up their unjust sales practices. These same merchants and tax collectors affixed Him to the cross and killed Him.

Today's merchants have also done a superb job of destroying the true meaning of Christmas. There are no more "specials" at Christmas for the children of this nation because what used to be Christmas specific merchandise is being sold all year long. The Christmas season is supposed to be a time to display full respect for Jesus Christ and his teachings. Instead, the merchants use it for a time to get more money in their cash registers and to hell with the holidays. And they didn't stop with Christmas. The merchants have done the same thing to Easter and Mother's Day. Their greed has put the almighty dollar above all else. We often wonder why the youth of America has lost respect for Christ and the church. Merchants are promoting this disrespect by their drive for profits 12 months out of the year.

It would appear that on Easter and Mother's Day the merchants would hand out flowers in the big stores to all the mothers to show their sincere appreciation to those mothers for shopping in their stores throughout the year. You never see this happening. What you do see is flowers for sale in these stores and to hell with thanking the mothers. It is also evident that the flowers in these stores are far more expensive that those sold on street corners. It seems the merchants do not even know how to say thank you to the mothers for their faithful patronage in the stores. Instead, they are baiting the mothers with sales. This is a disgrace for all American merchants.

REBATES

Rebates are nothing more than "sucker" bait. People who never had any money in their bank account might have a few bucks upon receipt of their rebate after buying a car. Why not just lower the price of the car and forget the rebates. I once bought oil for my car and had to mail in a request for a rebate to an area out of state. I sent the request by registered mail and have yet to receive my return receipt, although I did receive my 80 cents rebate. That was over 10 years ago.

Rebates are a rat race for sure, with most of the benefits being favorable to the sellers. Rebates should be done away with as soon as possible.

THE HIGH COST OF NASA

Let's hope that the flight crews for NASA go higher every time they take off. Maybe they will go high enough so God can punch them in the nose, and tell them "Stop snooping on me. Get back down to Earth and straighten out the vast mess America is in right now. I am running a clean operation (shop) and no way can you compare yours with mine."

I am not against NASA. I just feel that it should be financed by the big businessmen that profit from it and not the taxpayers. Let the businessmen foot the bill until the aircraft is ready for flight. There might be fewer delays in the flights if the businessmen were paying for them.

Americans have been told that people will be able to live in space in the near future. You can bet your last dollar that the American working class will never make one of those trips even though they are paying most of the bills to provide those living quarters. The "big boys" either get us into war in order to make big bucks or they give us NASA to pay for, which will still net them big bucks.

The United States now has so much to do on the ground that we hardly know where to start. I would recommend roads and bridges as a good place to start. I could list many more areas that merit at least as much attention and funding as NASA gets, but these two would be a good kick-off.

At present the working class and other taxpayers have to pay for the glory showered on NASA crews. This is unfair and the basic cost is just too high.

It would be very insightful if American women were talked into wearing hats again like they used to when I was a young boy. The men would, on Easter Sunday, pick up their wives hats and bring them to an open field for a hat throwing contest (not without a friendly bet on the side). The hat was given a sharp whip from the wrist and it was amazing what the hat could offer in flight. By the way, the hat contests were never put on hold.

MARRIAGES

Many marriages today are destined to fail. These failed marriages are a factor in the rising cost of attorney fees and other expenses. Divorce has become a big business for lawyers. Many Americans who are not divorced, and never plan to be, are forced to help pay for these failed marriages.

Divorce is much too easy to obtain in this country. When necessary, divorce is a family matter, not the concern of the governments. And it is the responsibility of the parents to accept what their children do or fail to do, regardless of the age of their children. Church leaders should be brought in to help people in troubled marriages. If the nation has to qualify more Parsons, then so be it. The people in charge of this now are not getting the job done.

It might be beneficial to have the backsides of marriage certificates imprinted with the saying "Kissing is fun, but marriage is a very serious business". There would certainly be nothing to lose by adding this "warning" to the backs of the certificates.

Something has to be done about the high rate of divorce in this country. Otherwise, all others will continue to carry the financial burden heaved upon them by the divorcees. It should be the responsibility of the parents of the divorcees to carry this burden. All marriages are not good, but all the marriages cannot be bad, either. It would be beneficial if the ones getting married were informed of the fact that a "true" marriage is achieved after the first hard disagreement.

Children of broken marriages are made to feel as misfits among their friends and are the ones who really have to rough it. We are told that the United States of America is a model for the rest of the world. In the area of marriage and divorce we are desperately lacking, and our children are proof of it.

From now on let's keep all government out of the marriage business. Children belong to their parents, not to the government.

When most Americans lived in rural communities a good country girl would not marry a man unless he smelled of hard work, owned a horse, and owed no debts (except for what was owed on the farm or ranch). It was also insured that the young man was not squatting to close to the house in case he had to be spared for war. There weren't many "quickies" in marriages then. The woman had to be spoken for and had to be promised to by the mother and father before the marriage could take place.

Pre-marital pregnancy was not a common thing back then either. The women in those days were well qualified on the use of a pitchfork. When the man became a little too fresh, a woman would put the pitchfork to his belly. As he turned to run she would strike his backside. Most men didn't return for a second try. Also, when the wife didn't get maximum results form her husband, she would march him, pitchfork in her hands, to the barn for the night and have the rats trim his toenails. One night in the barn was about all most husbands needed to shape up. Selling pitchforks again (and learning how to properly use them) might be a good idea for this country.

This is just another area that might cause God to raise his eyebrows on Judgement Day. He might say, "So many of you have been married so many times that I do not know which one of you is the right wife or husband".

THE AMERICAN SPORTS SYSTEM

To pay American professional athletes the money they are currently being paid is completely absurd. There are many Americans who do not like sports. These individuals unwillingly participate in the funding of professional sports because they use the commercial products endorsed by various professional sports clubs and/or athletes. The present system is a vast "sickie" at best, and should be abolished at once.

Professional athletes only "work" about six months per year. They are being paid the largest salaries in the nation for "playing", not "working". The sports announcers are also living high on the hog, with far too many on the job when one could do it by himself. To say the least, their "over-announcing" has made the game a very dull experience. Many times there are more words said before the pitch than there are stitches on a baseball. There is too much "bullstuff" in their announcing to cope with. They (the announcers) also like to meddle in others' business which, at times, is private. Yes, the announcers' booths nowadays are just too noisy.

It costs approximately $40 million to put on a boxing match in the heavy weight class. There are times when the fight only lasts one or two rounds. That is a lot of bucks for an obvious mismatch. Furthermore, the people cannot see the fight unless they pay additional money to the TV station broadcasting the match. Many of the football and baseball matches are no better.

Let us treat the sports programs henceforth like a business and pay the athletes with monies collected from the crowd who attend the games. (The 200 hitters would have to walk to and from the games.) Let us make it a true "game" from now on. No more ripping off those who could care less about the game. Don't get me wrong; I like sports, but only if they are provided on a true and honest basis. We do not have that scenario now. The people who are keeping America going are not making as much as the professional athlete's pocket change. If this blunder were corrected there would be more food for the stomachs of many.

Yes, a good policing of the professional sports system in America is long overdue. The paying of big money to support pine warmers and those standing on the sidelines is costly to the users of (professional sports) sponsors' products. In order to favor the people, the loud sound of the axe is long overdue here.

The shafting of Americans does not end here. There are many

ball players on American teams that came from Mexico, Puerto Rico and other countries. These ball players are taking big money out of this country. Many of these foreign ball players trained themselves on American foreign aid money while our young American former athletes worked to provide the foreign aid money.

I see no shortage of young American men to qualify for professional sports in this country. Let's discontinue the scuttling of our young American men by excluding from the games and fat payrolls. Professional club owners, whose side are you on? It's time to give our young men a long overdue break.

THE U.S. POSTAL SERVICE

In order to provide a much cheaper operation, the Federal Government should contract the postal service to a civilian contractor. By doing so, the Americans could be licking much cheaper stamps again. Furthermore, the mail would be delivered in a more timely manner. Currently the mail usually arrives at least one hour early on Saturdays and on the day prior to a holiday.

The present postal services are very costly. The postal employees are the same Federal Civil Service type who get a fat retirement check. Their hourly wage is much too high for the quality of work they do. There are many good hunters, fishermen, golfers, and happy hour participants among their ranks. The American people are now paying through the nose for the high cost of postal employees. Much of this high cost could be done away with if the postal operations were contracted out to the civilian sector. We have nothing to lose and everything to gain.

Our "buck passing" Congress established this costly postal operation, thereby excusing itself from financial responsibility associated with postal services.

HIGH COST OF DENTAL CARE

The cost of dental care in this country is far too high. For example, I had one spot filling (no injection needed) and had my teeth cleaned. The cost was over $90.00. Two weeks prior to my being treated, I took two dogs to the veterinarian for dental care. Both dogs had to be anesthetized for the treatment. The cost was $20.00. Between the two dogs they had 8 teeth extracted and the remainder of their teeth cleaned. The cost for this was $10.00.

Seven days of oral medication for the two dogs cost $6.00. The total bill = $36.00. By comparison of these two bills for treatment, it pays to be a dog nowadays in America.

Perhaps a barking school should be started for the people to learn how to bark. Maybe then we would get a break from the high cost of dental care. Going in barking and coming out growling would let them know the cost is too high.

Dentists are usually running behind time on their patients to boot. They usually have at least 2 or 3 chairs. The people with dental appointments should charge the dentist for being late. That would help to reduce the dental bill by some reasonable degree.

Perhaps we should return to the horse and buggy days. Back then the doctor had to care for the horse and the buggy, keep the stall free of droppings, and did not have time to write costly prescriptions. In those days St. Joseph aspirin usually got the job done with respect to medicinal needs. And those who thought they had it rough on the St. Joseph aspirin, well, many of us are still around today. The aspirin was called the mighty St. Joseph.

HEALTH CARE INSURANCE

Health care insurance companies are supposed to give complete coverage. The insurance companies rarely do until the renewal is received. The renewal boasts more complete coverage only if the recommended "extras" are added to the policy. It is a never ending rat race. This situation needs cleaning up at once. The American people deserve better from the insurance companies.

THE ECONOMY

Our American economy is only as good as the American industrial output. American businesses are now moving into Mexico and overseas, and the "one-sided" foreign trade is putting Americans out of work. This is simply not indicative of a healthy economy.

Many Americans are unable to find a job and in some cases, where it is needed, they are unable to find a second job. This is not good economy. When high school and college seniors do not have a job waiting for them upon graduation. This is not good economy. When those who are working still have to depend on food stamps to make ends meet. This is not good economy.

Many Americans now have to go against their will and pride to provide a "credit card" Christmas, Easter, Thanksgiving, etc. This is not good economy. Many people sell items at flea markets and yard sales to try to make a few bucks; items that were once given away to charitable organizations. This is not good economy.

Nowadays in America there are a large number of bankruptcies and foreclosures. Some good Americans have been forced to steal just to have something to eat. This is not good economy.

The lumber production in this country has had to take a back seat to the spotted owl and other stupid practices. This is not good economy. Perhaps the Vice President will show the American people how to make and eat soup from owl droppings with the President looking on.

Many cement factories in the nation are now a home for spiders, mice and rats because of the one-sided foreign trade putting Americans out of work. Americans are compelled to buy foreign products instead of products "Made in America". When Americans have to sell coffee grown in foreign countries (putting Americans out of work). That is just bad economy.

The pollution in America is being overplayed by the snoops and sniffers in Washington. This is driving the American businesses out of the country, and putting thousands out of work. If the $4 trillion debt has not killed us, the pollution could very well be good for us all.

The once bountiful American fruit orchards are now growing grass and weeds. The American fruit growers are required to comply with all sorts of regulations, whereby their foreign competitors are not required to comply with the same strict standards. The small Mexican fly, for example, will send many in Washington up into the clouds. But they will ignore the American fruit growers, again putting Americans out of work. This is not good economy.

The American beer companies have been given a big bashing by the foreign beer industries, putting Americans out of work. Many Americans are now compelled to wear shoes made in foreign countries (mine were made in China). Now I am hearing that there might not be one leather factory in the United States. This practice is putting thousands of Americans out of work. This is not good economy.

The once good paying jobs in the American automobile industry have now moved out of the country, putting Americans out of work. Most radio and TV sets are now being manufactured in countries overseas, putting Americans out of work. This is just not good economy and the American workers continue to pay the price for it.

PAY RAISES AND COST OF LIVING ADJUSTMENTS (COLA)

Government pay raises and cost of living adjustments (COLA) should be frozen for the time being. This includes the Congress and Senate and other top government workers. If pay raises and COLA are to be continued, they should be a flat rate across the board for all Americans. If the small wage earners have to make it on, for example, $25 per month increase, then everyone else should be made to dance to the same music. I think it would be better to freeze the prices instead.

Under our current system, the rich initiate the pay raises then increase the prices on products, and in the end pocket the profits. As a result, the low wage earners and those on fixed incomes play a never ending game of catch the rabbit. It is a game played on the underdogs. To date no overall gain can be seen from it.

Let's give small wage earners a break because, in most cases, they are the ones who are keeping America going. In the military ranks it is the privates, E-1 through E-5, who are keeping the other soldiers happy and smiling. It is pretty much the same in the civilian sector.

Redesigning the pay raises and COLA could save the taxpayers a ton of money. Let's stop fattening the wallets of the biggies. It is not uncommon for them to hold a position of rank that is not even necessary. Stopping this injustice on the taxpayers is long overdue.

JOBS FOR AMERICANS THAT ONCE WERE

If the gasoline companies were made to do away with the self-service gas pumps, many jobs would return to the people like they once were. When we paid 18 cents for a gallon of gas the attendant on the job checked the oil, checked the tires and aired them when needed, checked the radiator and filled it if necessary, cleaned the glass on all the windows and vacuumed the inside of the car when needed. These services were free. The price for the gasoline was much better then, too. The person on the job displayed a pleasing and courteous attitude to the customer. He also had a great deal of technical knowledge about cars and would share this knowledge for free of charge. All of these services were offered when we paid just 18 cents per gallon for gasoline.

Now we pay over $1 per gallon for gasoline. We pump the gas ourselves with a nozzle that feels like a sawed-off shotgun in our hands. Many extra services can be had, but only with an additional charge. The person on the job at the gas stations is usually a young woman who does not know the workings of a car from the workings of a cow, loaded with "I do not knows".

Yes, many jobs could be restored here if the gasoline companies were made to serve the people like they once were served at gas stations.

Store owners used to deliver a customer's purchases to their homes without extra cost. If that practice was restored many jobs would return to the people again. Many other businesses could put people on the job like they once did. All too often businesses cut the work force at every chance they get instead of hiring more people to maintain an acceptable level of service. In most cases where businesses cut the work force the services are lousy at best.

UNITED STATES AMBASSADORS

The Ambassadors appointed for assignments abroad must be qualified to represent the United States of America in all aspects. The present procedure of merely representing their party is not getting any job done. For example, the Ambassador to Iraq was asleep on the job. They have to be business all the way, and see to it that foreign aid monies reach those the money was intended for. They can no longer be appointed to these posts to lie, connive, and live high on the hog. They give the impression that all Americans live as they do and that in America money grows on trees in the summer and falls from the sky in winter.

Henceforth we should insure the Ambassadors are personnel who worked hard for their living in America; people who will always put America first in their dealings with foreign nations. We do not have Ambassadors of this caliber now. The appointing of "fine ole boys and girls" as Ambassadors has been counter-productive since the end of WWII. This is not the place nor the time for any more free rides.

America can no longer afford to assign chair warmers to the

very important posts of Secretary and/or Ambassador. Those appointed will have to fight for America from now on or we will be taken over by foreign countries. This responsibility goes with the job.

Let us not forget there are many babies born everyday in America and they, too, will have to be employed some day. From now on this is not the place or time for "Mr. Nice Guys" and "Ms. Nice Gals". Their support of Presidents for re-election has proven, in some cases, to be a losing battle because the Presidents were voted out of office on election day. From now on the Ambassadors and Secretaries should do the job they were appointed to do and let the President prove his worth in his job like he was elected to do.

Henceforth, let us have the Ambassadors and the Secretaries show us wear and tear on their clothes other than that found on the seat of their pants and skirts. And don't any of you be afraid to go down swinging for your country.

SECRETARIES OF LABOR

The main job of the Secretary of Labor is to defend, in all cases, every possible job for the American people. They certainly must have turned their head, as well as a deaf ear, when (before their very eyes) the American companies started moving overseas and into Mexico, taking American jobs with them. The Secretary should have been shouting, "What are you trying to do to my working class and the nation?" Not one word was heard, nor did we see one punchout.

All of the secretaries have been on the American payroll. For what? The Secretary of Labor was not heard from November, 1993 when the (shameful) NAFTA was being debated on television. On whose side is the Secretary? All of the secretaries should be required to go to the graduating seniors of high schools and colleges to point out where the good paying jobs are waiting for them, now and in the future. It would be a good idea if they took along the ones who voted yes on NAFTA to weigh the damage their "yes" vote did for the nation. One cannot fool facts.

We, as American workers, have not been getting the service we deserve from the Secretary of Labor in many years. Employment for the American people should always be the Secretary's number one business. The Secretary needs to show more concern for the American people and he must show it now.

If the present trend continues, America will not be able to defend herself. Furthermore, the United States military star rank officers, instead of going to American industrial colleges, will have to go to Mexico and overseas to beg for supplies. It is not a pretty picture.

While all this wheeling and dealing has taken place, the Secretary of Defense not been heard from.

THE SECRETARY OF AGRICULTURE

Since the conclusion of WWII those appointed as Secretaries of Agriculture have not been fighting (standing up) for the American farmers, ranchers, and poultry and hog farmers like they have been expected to. At present, several country musicians and a handful of others have been trying to point out to Washington that the "home" folks have been neglected by the Secretary of Agriculture. The Secretary is on our payroll. It appears that the Secretary might not want to disappoint the big wheelers and dealers in Washington, allowing our people to go broke and forcing them out of the farming business. Many American farms have become a home for insects, birds, wild animals, mice and rats. These farms grow weeds and show shame instead of farm products.

Any nation without a good farm system is not a sound nation. This is a double hit for the taxpayers because they have to pay the farmers not to farm, as well as funding unemployment benefits for the unemployed.

The present standards are sick at best. Only a qualified farmer or rancher should be appointed to the very important post of Secretary of Agriculture. The city boys do not know straight up about a cow. One even had to be shown how to pat a hog and cow on the back. Yes, there are far better men for the job than that.

Furthermore, agricultural aid from the American government sent to foreign governments is putting American people out of business. The American people are getting the shaft. This is not good for the future of our nation.

SECRETARY OF TRANSPORTATION

The Secretary of Transportation wants to sleep on the job, allowing the once very effective railroad system to be almost taken over by the trucking companies. This is extremely costly by comparison and not nearly as efficient. A nation without good rail transportation is standing on one leg.

If we were now using rail transportation, the food products and other goods would be much cheaper to buy. Europe and Japan both have good rail systems and their nations appear more complete in the area of transportation.

The rail tracks in this country appear to be hungry for maintenance. It is very shameful to hear and to see where the American trains are falling from tracks when we have people out of work in the thousands that could be hired to fix them. Instead, we waste money on food stamps.

Had it not been for the efficient railroad system in WWII, there is no way America could have been prepared not only to fight, but to win the "big" war in 3 years, 8 months, and 25 days. Trucks are only a drip-of-the-faucet by efficiency comparison.

If the trains were restored back to the tracks, prices would go down for the good of all in this country. Lack of foresight in Washington is causing America now to cope with a very costly transportation system that is less efficient and less dependable.

It is time to hear more train whistles in America.

CAR INSURANCE

Individuals that keep a car for 20 years pay for it twice; they pay once for the base price of the car and they pay a second time by keeping the car insured. Just because a person <u>might</u> have an accident doesn't mean he will actually be in one. Furthermore, many teenagers drive better than some of the older population. Yet, teenagers must pay a higher price for auto insurance simply because of their age. The insurance premiums should be based on whether or not an accident has occurred.

Under the present system the auto insurance companies cannot lose. The insurance companies always give the appearance they are doing the people a big favor. They never ask, "Can you afford the insurance policy?". They are a "deep pocket" outfit. Let the insurance company buy all the used cars from the people. That would leave their eyes wide open.

PROPERTY INSURANCE

The insurance companies never sell a complete policy until it is time to renew the policy. At the time of renewal the insurance company lists many "extras" that give more protection. Insured property under the present system is not completely covered. For example, property damaged by a car requires that <u>you</u> pay a deductible. The deductible should be paid by the individual causing the damage (or by his insurance company). This is not the case now.

Since the insurance companies think that they are not over charging policy holders, we should let them try buying all the properties from the sellers and resell them. This also holds true for property tax collectors. Let the county courthouse buy properties from the sellers and resell them. Both the insurance companies and the tax collectors would change their tunes, but fast!

HIGH COST OF SUPPLEMENTAL INSURANCE TO MEDICARE

The companies selling Medicare supplemental insurance have no mercy on the American people. These supplements cost anywhere from $50 to $100 per month. This is why some of the 37 million people in America do not have health care insurance on themselves right now. If an elderly person is worth one year's value of supplements, then I could be sold for $1,200. The elderly in America are worth more than that.

There are entirely too many insurance companies in the health care business, with some companies lacking the financial backing to process all claims. One thing, for sure, can be said about the U.S. Government in Washington, D.C. They (the government) have turned the American people over to the insurance company "sharks" instead of having a suitable health care policy for them.

The 537 elected officials in Washington, D.C. do not have to cope like the average American does. The elected officials have complete health coverage paid for by the American people. They also have the U.S. Navy on standby 24 hours a day. America is supposed to be a nation of equal opportunity. It is not. Let us drink from the same cup for a change. True equality is long overdue in this nation.

AMERICAN LABOR UNIONS

Unions accomplished a great deal for the American workers when they were first formed. It wasn't long, though, before they became hungry for money and began to hurt the workers instead of helping them. Since the conclusion of WWII there have been too many strikes. The workers have lost too much time on these strikes and have made very little headway on the original ideals of the unions.

The unions' greed for money and higher wages for the workers has split the American way of life. Those on minimum wage and those working part time jobs are unable to make ends meet. Many American companies have beat it to Mexico or overseas to find a cheap source of labor. The government in Washington should have denied these companies the "OK" to ship these jobs away from American workers. This movement of American jobs to foreign countries will undoubtedly harm the future of our nation and, therefore, its people.

American businesses approve of this overseas movement of jobs because it provides them with a cheap labor source and the ability to sell their products at an all time high profit margin. It is totally wrong for these businesses to shaft the nation and its people in the name of higher profit. In a few years time the countries allowing American industries into them will become number one while the United States will become number two, or even further down the line. The United States is no longer the self-sustaining nation it claimed to be a number of years ago.

I am not anti-union. I just feel their ultimate goal should be to unite, not divide. The American businesses now in Mexico and overseas should be made to return to the United States, or be dissolved. For those businesses choosing to dissolve, replacement businesses could be created right here on American soil.

The American working class, not cheap foreign labor, made the big businessmen what they are today. Before, and during, WWII America took a backseat to no one. Period. This is how we won WWII. The free world looked up to us. It's not the same situation anymore.

For all their valiant efforts the American workers never received a word of thanks. Instead, the businessmen used deceit (to hide the real truth) by telling their workers there was a need to cut cost(s) in the operations. Surely at this moment God is expanding the space in hell to reserve room for these businessmen when the time comes for their judgement day.

The United States is now standing on one leg where the American worker is concerned. America (Big Mom) is looking for a better tomorrow because under the present system she cannot sustain herself. The unions need to police their operations to better fit the real needs of the American workers. An effort should be made to bring what was once American jobs back into this country. The wage gap(s) of American workers could use some scrutiny. The facts cannot be fooled. The time to act is now, before it is too late for America and its people.

SECRETARY OF EDUCATION

Education in America has become a joke. To correct the problem, several issues need to be resolved. To begin with, all schools should use the same textbooks for the respective grades. This is the only way parents can be assured their children are receiving the same level of learning as children in other schools. If all the schools used the same set of textbooks it would give the American education system the solid foundation it needs. This would go a long way in correcting the second problem. The fact that many parents, both civilian and military, often have to uproot their children to move with their careers. This inevitably causes hardship on the children in the area of education. Once the move is completed the children must face a whole new set of textbooks. If all the school used the same educational materials, these children would slide easily into the same routine of learning.

The present education system is "left-legged" and that means it stands for no direction. I suggest, Mr. Secretary, that you teach school for three months per year to get a handle on what it takes to keep the education system of this nation moving in a positive direction. I believe there is a surprise waiting, should you take my suggestion. The education system is no place for guess work.

TEACHERS

American students need the best teachers our nation can provide. All teachers should be tested to insure their level of proficiency, with all 50 states using the same testing materials. A background check should be required with an emphasis on morals, devotion to duty, and financial status. Only those who put America and the welfare of their students first would be considered.

Teachers should not close schools for the purpose of holding meetings. Meetings should be held in the evenings, on weekends and during the summer months. Teachers who send children home without books (homework) should have to explain to the parents why the children have no work to do. The teachers who go on strike should lose their teaching certificates and lose their privilege to teach forever.

Teachers should not forget that when the schools are closed for meetings the parents have to spend money on baby-sitters. If it weren't for the students the teachers would have no job. I suggest the teachers cut out the "horsestuff" and get down to the very serious business of education.

Too many teachers put money above teaching and the welfare of their students. This has caused many of the school children to lose faith in the schools and their desire to learn.

I recommend the teachers learn a lesson from the military. The education and care of young soldiers is put above all else. When teachers learn to do the same for their students they will begin to see a greater efficiency in their work. The time has come for teachers to treat their job as an honor, not as a hardship. The hard work needed to be done by our teachers should be fun and rewarding for them.

DRESS CODES

Too many of our students nowadays look out of place in the classroom. A dress code is needed in our schools to let the students know how they are supposed to look. All too often it is the students dressed in a poor fashion (whether they can afford better clothing or not) that prove to be the trouble makers. The clothing merchants will howl but we'll just have to let them howl.

A dress code should also be required for the teachers. Some of the female teachers dress in much too casual a fashion for school in the summer months. Having a dress code for the teachers would also set a good example for the students to follow.

Most private schools have a dress code. Their dress code is a big factor in their success with the students. Dressing in a neat fashion instills pride and responsibility in the students as well as a healthy respect for others.

The dress code for our schools does not have to be an elaborate one. A simple, but presentable, code would be sufficient. In order to be fair, the dress code should be the same for all 50 states.

STUDENT TROUBLE MAKERS

Putting student trouble makers under control should pose no problem, yet we continue to hear the excuse that there aren't enough funds for use in school discipline enforcement. School administrators now outnumber the teachers. If we fired 85% of the administrators we could use that payroll funding to hire school guards to enforce the discipline. The guards could police the arrival and departure of students, making sure no one enters the campus that doesn't belong there and no one leaves without proper permission. The guards could also "shake down" the students for weapons and have the parents remove the violators from the school.

Teachers often find it difficult to teach with the volume of administrators in our schools looking over their shoulders. By downsizing the number of administrators it would allow our teachers to become good teachers again, without the stress of administrative meddling.

Students are seeing the weaknesses in school discipline and are taking full advantage of them. The problem we have is not so big that it cannot be controlled. It is simply that the policy is too weak to control the students.

If letting go of 85% of the administrators does not gain enough funding for guards, then more resources could be had by firing the sports teachers. That should provide the needed funds to get the job done. If, after these suggestions, the job still cannot be accomplished by the few administrators left, we should fire them. There are many Americans out there who can get the job done if they were just given the chance.

Problems are like babies; both grow large when nursed. There is no problem too big to handle if it is tackled properly and in a timely manner.

BUSSING STUDENTS

Making students walk to and from school would be good for them. It wouldn't hurt the soft and lazy ones. In fact, it would teach them responsibility and make them better Americans when they grow up.

The school administrators should be made to drive the busses we do have now. The responsibility (and fresh air) would be good for them, too. The motto should be: Don't let your college degree get in your way or you will be replaced.

Once control is established in our schools, the serious students will be most grateful. The parents will be thankful as well. The present "good ole boy" system has failed us. Success can happen with the right kind of people on the job.

CARS AND HIGH SCHOOL STUDENTS

Seventy-five percent of the control problems of students could be eliminated by denying the students the ability to drive their cars to school. This would also be a nice break for the city police as they would no longer have to monitor the students driving to and from school. Students would return to their homes after school instead of cruising all over town. The only cars allowed on school grounds should be for the teachers. Those who scream about their rights being violated should be dismissed form school. Taxpayers are funding school bills for the students to show good report cards, not fancy cars.

Teachers should not have to deal with the problems associated with the current policy of students and their cars. These problems should be dealt with by the parents.

Many students drive to town to play video game machines. These machines should be put off limits to the students on school days. This would be a great help to the teachers and to Mom and Dad. The game machine owners could care less about the students, only that they put their money in his pockets.

If parents and teachers could count on the cooperation of video machine owners a lot could be accomplished with regards to controlling students in America.

SEX EDUCATION IN SCHOOLS

Parents should have the responsibility of teaching their children sex education, not our teachers. In fact, schools (or any other public area) is no place for the word "sex" to be permitted to be heard. Once the students get worked up in school about sex, they will go home and try it out. It makes it very convenient to the student when both parents are working.

Teaching sex education in the schools makes the students appear less than an animal. Animals need no instruction in the area of sex. The present policy on sex education is destroying the efforts of those families who are giving it their best shot to raise their children right. Let's not forget that sex education in the schools does, in many cases, create a "wild herd" effect among the young boys and girls. America was built by those who practiced high moral standards, not by a wild herd.

Many of today's parents could stand some education themselves in the areas of high morals and sex discipline. The wild herd is too large in this country and, as you well know, a wild herd does not make a good herd. We no longer hear a young man say he married a virgin, nor that the young woman married a saint. Those days are gone because of the low moral standards in many of today's homes and by the public teaching of sex education in our schools.

LYING TO STUDENTS

Many of our high school students are being lied to when they are promised a job upon graduation from college. There is no job that will wait for them for four years. There simply are not that many jobs available in this country. Currently many of our college graduates have to take a job that entails selling foreign products to Americans. This should not be happening.

Often times our college graduates have to take unskilled jobs like shoveling sheep droppings in Idaho, Montana, or Wyoming. (This should not be misconstrued as a smirk at these states because all three are superb states in every respect.) In many cases when the graduates do have to take a low paying job it is because the school from which they graduated failed to properly assist them in or prepare them for finding a job.

I suggest that the job market be thoroughly tested before assigning the students to degree programs. The present system for students is a hit and miss policy (with more misses than hits).

There is no substitute for the truth when it comes to spending the taxpayer's money on education.

SCHOLARSHIPS

Scholarships are another area to be considered when it comes to wasting tax dollars. All Americans now contribute to the education of each student in this country. It should be the responsibility of the parent to see that their child gets an education. Of course, the elected ones in the state and federal capitols make it look like they care about education, but their "caring" is merely bait for another vote.

Scholarship money should be granted only to those students who are at or near the top of their schools in their academics. No more money for athletic scholarships.

Money spent on worthwhile scholarships is money spent on good, solid, book learning. This is scholarship money that will show positive results for the future of America. Our current system is a costly one with shoddy results produced for the money being spent. Let's clean up the "free ride" policy and get down to serious business when spending the taxpayer's money from now on.

PEOPLE IN WASHINGTON

Officials in Washington are unaware of the severity of problems in public schools because their children attend private schools. The Secretary of Education is not getting the job done by merely showing his face on TV. In all aspects of school operations there is no place for a "fine ole boy".

Many homes in America are functioning with low moral standards. The teaching of sex education in the schools is promoting that illicit sex is no longer a sin, but is recreation instead. This is dangerous to the moral fiber of our nation.

When parents are held responsible for everything their children do (or fail to do), the schools will see a noticeable improvement in all areas.

SPORTS IN HIGH SCHOOLS

All parents should not be made to participate in the financing of sports activities in our high schools. Only those parents who wish to have their children participate in the sports programs (on Friday and Saturday night) should have to pay. This is another area that is deterring learning in our schools. Many of our high school athletes are granted scholarships not for their learning ability, but for how fast they can run, jump, etc. The athletes are getting the big attention in our colleges, while the exceptional learners are taking a back seat to the athletes or not mentioned at all.

Taxpayers should not be made to fund the athletic events. The primary mission of our schools should be education, not sports. Our present preoccupation with sports in the schools is doing a great deal of damage to the learning process in our schools.

If the professional teams want to continue to play on Friday nights, let them pay the bills. This also goes for the ones who claim the poorer ones cannot compete. The current sports system is long overdue for a swift kick in the butt. Sports programs being kicked completely off high school campuses for good wouldn't be a bad idea either.

AMERICAN LAW ENFORCEMENT PERSONNEL

In the present time, all too often everybody is right but the American lawmen. Many of the people violating the law are getting away with it because all they have to say is "my rights were violated". If that person had not broken the law, the police officer would not have had to make contact with him or her. It is evident that violators of the law receive more media attention than do the law enforcement personnel. This is not a situation which is favorable to our nation.

It is the responsibility of parents to teach their children to obey the law and to show respect to law enforcement personnel at all times. Children should be kept off the streets after a certain time. It is also the responsibility of the parents to see that their children are properly disciplined when the children do behave in an unacceptable manner where law and law enforcement officers are concerned. Officers of the law are not the children's parents and have other, important things to do in their line of work. The bottom line is this. Parents have a moral and legal obligation to control their children.

When my friends and I were youngsters all a police officer would have to do was look at us and we would quickly straighten up. A slap on the jaw by a police officer was not uncommon and would end 95% of the minor problems, saving a lot of time and money avoiding arrests and court costs. We'd never let our parents find out we were involved in an episode with a police officer or we would have caught a full payload of hell for at least a week.

There are times today when parents are unable to discipline their children because of aimless lawyers out looking for a few easy bucks. These lawyers are promoting violence and a growing disrespect for the law enforcement personnel.

Law enforcement personnel now have the most dangerous job in our nation, with insufficient appreciation for all their dangerous efforts. Their job can be compared to fighting a war without a victory for the troops. Our law enforcement officers are on a battlefield every day with no better end in sight for them to look forward to.

The state and federal capitols have let this law enforcement personnel "bashing" get out of hand. It is unsafe to be an American nowadays, regardless of when and where. Those who support the violence should be jailed with the law violators. Our motto should be "Good Americans do not break the law".

Of course, our law makers in Washington make laws for us to follow, then fail to follow the laws themselves. This promotes a "Why should the rest of us have to follow the rules?" attitude. This injustice aggravates the problem of violence in this country. It is time for the "Big Boys and Girls" in Washington to lead this nation by setting a worthy example for us to follow.

POSITIVE POLICY AND PROCEDURE AS A GUIDE FOR ALL AMERICANS

It would be so much simpler for the United States court system if we had instructions like those found in the Military Court Martial Manuals for all to follow. Each of the 50 states should use the same instructions and train people in the same manner for jury duty, with lawyers required to sit on jury duty as well. Court cases should be contracted to lawyers with suspense dates for completion. And above all, let the new manual state that our Congress must abide by all laws just like all other Americans must do.

A few new rules could only help the current system. Why not have the parents pay for their children's jail time and their meals? Or have the law violator's family pay for the victim's burial and other bills since the victim was not at fault. Treat runaway fathers (and mothers) as the criminals they are, and punish those who hide the runaways, including those who hide foreign nationals.

Those who disagree with the verdict should be fined and jailed because laws are written to be obeyed equally by all. Sympathizing in support of law violators should itself be a crime and punishable by law. Lawyers should pay for appeals. This alone should save the taxpayers some big bucks.

Laws should be tougher than the criminals. When the criminals want to match the law, let them pay the price. Laws and what they pertain to should be specific. List exactly what is a case of rape. Touching a woman on the knee should not be considered rape.

The new manual should point out to those Americans that deal with foreign countries that they are committing treason. This would certainly put the easy buck makers in line, like they should be, if we are to have the dependability that is long overdue for this nation. No more shafting of Americans by Americans.

There should be no more money from taxpayers or foreign nations for re-election campaigns. Unless this is ended, America will continue to march out of step. Let our officials run for re-election on their past duty accomplishments or they can go home as losers. The present policies regarding re-elections are costly, with no apparent benefit to the American people, and are getting worse every day.

The new manual should make it known that our Congress was elected to serve the nation and its people. Currently the people are the ones serving the Congress and our forefathers did not establish a Congress for the people to serve. Our Congressmen are paid to lead by example in all aspects. If all Americans behaved like so many of our Congressmen do, we would have no America. The nation would be buried by misuse and wrongdoing. One duty should be specified for the Vice President and that is to run herd on the Congress. If he does not carry out this responsibility, he can go home without any retirement due to him. This should also be happen to all elected officials that violate the laws.

All Americans should have the same kind of birth certificate, regardless of the color of their skin. America is a nation of equal opportunity, so it is being said. It should be looked upon as an honor to be an American. The good people of the USA should have no problems living here.

Our nation continues to scratch its head wondering how to fight crime in a constructive way. To begin with we could have all 50 states use the same instructions for their prisons. This would eliminate most of the confusion.

State governors and city mayors should be responsible for the control of drugs, crime, and all other violations. Have officials in Washington D.C. show the way by cleaning up the D.C. area as a model for the nation to follow.

No more free rides should be allowed for property owners. Rental property owners should shoulder the responsibility of keeping drugs off of their property. In the event an ambulance or fire truck must be called, let the law violator responsible for the call be made to pay the bill, otherwise the cost should be paid by the rental property owner. I often see fire trucks or an ambulance going to some local rental property. The property owners are never seen. The good property owners are tired of paying for their lousy operations and control of their rental personnel. The responsibility lies with the rental property owner.

The instruction manual should also make it clear that the drug dealers on the street will be rewarded if they tell where the drugs are coming from. This way the big boys supplying the drugs can be rounded up.

The manual should state that officials messing around with our Social Security System will be booted out of Washington. Social Security is not a game for them to play, and must be treated with utmost respect as the serious business it is. Enough is enough.

The Bible reads that those who kill must be killed. Once I was in the Middle East on assignment. While I was there a soldier shot and killed an army officer around 0800 hours. Both the officer and the soldier that killed him were buried that same day. I was informed by one of the locals that their country did not treat crime as a business like we do in the United States. This rule from the Bible should be included in the manual.

Good soldiers in the military like the Court Martial Manual because it protects their rights and renders them safety. The same kind of manual could be as effective for the good Americans in the civilian sector. I do not feel that America should be a police state. This is not the case. I just feel it is unsafe to be an American nowadays. Clear and positive instructions, for all Americans to comply with, are needed to have the trust and safety our nation once had, and are long overdue. Our nation now has more laws than there are law enforcement personnel. Weak laws in America are inviting crime and smirks from law violators. The present conditions are no good for our nation.

NORTH AMERICAN FREE TRADE AGREEMENT (NAFTA)

I watched the NAFTA wheeling and dealing TV in November, 1993. It produced a full payload of shame for America and its people. It became another sellout of our nation and people. Those elected in Washington were out-numbered by those who voted "yes" on NAFTA. America swallowed another shame. I wish the American people could receive half as much support in their needs from the government in Washington. The government gave their best shot to please Mexico and left the American people wishing for better tomorrows.

The elected ones were saying that the time is upon the United States to break away from isolation. Hell! America has been isolated by the foreigners since the end of WWII by the Marshall Plan. They are still giving the United States a severe shafting in the one-sided foreign trade. Now who is isolated? It surely is not the United States who is doing the isolating. The "Made in America" label is hard to find in this country nowadays.

Furthermore, the pitch was made in the NAFTA debate concerning the American cars the Mexican people will buy. That pitch won't work because to believe you could buy an American car on $1.48 per hour is a very foolish way of thinking. It also indicates a lack of know-how on what it takes to make a living away from Washington.

Those who voted yes on NAFTA (allowing American businesses to slip away to Mexico and overseas) are not being heard telling the American high school and college graduates that there is good paying jobs waiting for them. Most of the officials in Washington do not even know where the unemployment offices are located in their own hometowns. Talk is cheap, especially in Washington and in state capitols. The officials are not seen talking to those who have lost their jobs because their company moved to Mexico or overseas. That one could bring in a bloody nose or full blown punchout.

Those who voted "yes" on NAFTA should be made to make plans for the mothers and wives for 15 and 30 days each month. They would quickly realize it is not easy for those who live away from Washington. With the present setup, there are no bad days in Washington regarding receiving a paycheck every month. Many start with the same monthly pay, even though they have no knowledge of the job. Yes, things are very different away from Washington when it comes to making a living.

It would also be very insightful for those who voted on NAFTA to spend their time away from Washington in El Paso, Texas, with the winds blowing in from the south. The stinking winds would have plenty of everything in them. It would be a very good teacher for them and they would not vote "yes" on another NAFTA styled agreement again. Never take a chance because you have a short nose.

At present there is no (sound) stability of jobs in America because of all the catering to Mexico and other foreign nations. The sick thing about it is the products made in foreign countries are costing us more than we use to pay for them "Made in the USA". It is a deep pocket operation by our businessmen. It makes one wonder how God will handle them on judgement day. He just might throw them into hell on top of Josef Stalin.

IMMIGRANTS

The time has come for the United States government in Washington (and the state capitols) to close the gates, rivers, and shores that are now open to immigrants. The immigrants today are not the same as those who were instrumental in building America. Today's immigrants are getting a free ride, and a very costly one at that. Taxpayers finance approximately $35 billion per year for the benefit and care of immigrants. Most immigrants are better cared for than the Americans who work to support them. If the elected officials in Washington want to continue to allow the current immigration standards, let them pay for the bills from their own bank accounts.

America is already overpopulated from its own stock and has no need for immigrants. Limiting immigrants in our nation could also help reduce unemployment. The current food stamp recipients in America could be employed in farming/agricultural jobs, many of which are now filled by immigrants. This would also help the Americans realize a new respect for the farm products and what the farmers must do to feed the American people. We have everything to gain here and nothing to lose.

The current volume of immigration must be stopped. Our nation has no shortage of people. America can no longer be used as a dumping ground for foreigners that can not or will not be cared for by their home nations. The "Halt" command is long overdue here, with stiff penalties needed for those who infringe on it by hiding illegal immigrants.

ANCESTORS

Many Americans want to support the countries their ancestors came from. This is a personal matter and should be treated as such. All Americans should not be made to support the current procedures and policies. There are some individuals now who are howling loudly in support of the ancestors, but are not working to help pay the bills concerning them.

From this point on let's treat the ancestor funding like the personal choice it should be. The good Americans (good doers) are tired of the present fallacy and are looking forward to the officials in Washington putting a stop to the unfair funding of support of the ancestors.

THE FUTURE OF AMERICA

The late Walter Winchell said it best when WWII ended: "To put Germany and Japan in the same footing with the United States, in about 40 years they will be telling the United States of America what to do or not to do." He hit the nail square on the head. The future of America is at stake here. I think that finally the United States Government in Washington, D.C. is beginning to see the light.

Japan is buying businesses (and land) in the United States left and right. In a few years they will own us all. We give them foreign aid and they use it to buy us out. This is not in the best interest for our nation. I am not sure how much Germany (and other nations) are buying in America, but a halt needs to come to these practices. The American (government) fools will do anything for money and to hell with the nation and its people.

Japan is the country most guilty of giving America the shaft as far as being one-sided in trade. The time has come for the United States to tell them to give us back what we are giving them so we will all be happy. This demand for equality is long overdue.

Japan is not the only country buying America out. There are many other countries, such as Mexico, doing the same thing. Our government in Washington is supposed to be on guard against such operations. Some of the "Good Ole Boys" are actually promoting the buy out in America instead of denying the foreign countries' opportunity for the sale. Legislation should be enacted so we would have protection for Americans and their land from foreign investment and laws to punish those who seek foreign investment. Let's protect America and its property like it used to be.

The "Made in America" label, our factories and other American resources whipped their butts in WWII. America has now been so gutted that it would be impossible to repeat our WWII victory. The Americans have been made to feel second best, or even less, and they certainly have not asked for it. This status has been forced upon them by the officials in Washington. Our nation and her people have earned and deserve better from our government.

About 25 years ago I spoke with two men from Europe. Our conversation was centered on the treatment of the American people by our government in Washington. Both of the Europeans said that their countrymen treat their dogs better than the government treats its people here in the United States.

If we are to still be a nation 50 years from now, a thorough house cleaning by the American voters is necessary. The American people are the ones who will have to eliminate the wheeling and dealing in Washington. We must pass laws as soon as possible to put an end to the present wrongdoing.

THE PRESIDENT

REFORMING THE GOVERNMENT IN WASHINGTON IS LONG OVERDUE. THE COUNTRY BELONGS TO THE PEOPLE, NOT WASHINGTON

The President should serve all the people equally. The present policy of being the President for one party is not getting the job done. The President should be elected as a statesman, not a party member. The President and Vice President should serve their four year terms as a service to the nation, without compensation. Current procedures for electing the President has split our nation in half, and this is not good for our country.

The President should appoint his Vice President to the position of Chief of Staff. There should be a 50/50 split of Republicans and Democrats in his cabinet. The current party appointments are like placing a bet on a one-legged man in a butt kicking contest. No chances to win. The President should also remain in his office to do the work he was elected to do. No more globe-trotting like we have seen since the 1960's.

Our President should face the nation and its people and always put them first. He should thoroughly understand the country's business from A to Z and attend all foreign trade meetings himself, along with the Secretary of Labor. These meetings are no place for the uneducated people we have been sending. They have already got us into trouble with their lack of know-how. The present system is not working and has failed America and her people.

After reform, the President will see to it that there will be no more money rendered to any of the elected ones to run for reelection: not from the government, the American people, Mexico, or from any country abroad. They will have to get reelected on their job performance ar they can go home as losers. Only a small amount of government funds will be used for first time elections. No more will elections be purchased in this country. This change is long overdue.

We need a President who will be able to get the job done without sending the U.S. Military Forces to a small rabbit shoot like we had in Kuwait or to haul food to the hungry in some foreign country. We need a President who will return the military forces back to military control so taxpayers can be proud of them again. After all, it is the taxpayers paying the bills. Under the present policy, the eager young military personnel are pointing fingers at the ground where once highly disciplined and properly led forces marched and trained.

We need a President who will put a stop to the current policy in the military allowing personnel to claim foreign parents as dependents. The dependents have priority over military retirees and their dependents. On whose side is Washington? Perhaps all the military retirees should have their name changed to a foreign one so they can get a fair shake where military medical benefits are concerned. Talk about a free ride; this is surely one. The elected ones in Washington do not have to deal with such policies. We really need a change for the better here.

The President needs to appoint real people to the Secretary positions. People who have worked for a living, such as picking cotton, operated a sledge hammer, or worked for minimum wage. Those that have worked in the corn fields and on wheat threshers, walked to and from work, ate sandwiches for lunch and know good work clothes could do the job. And let's not forget those that have served in the military in combat type units or others who have stood in unemployment lines. These are the people that need a real say in our Government.

The White House Chaplain can stop praying for the Congress and Senate. All they have shown us is a debt of $4 trillion (and growing). Instead, let the Chaplain pray for the American mothers who are keeping America afloat. To pay a chaplain over $100,000 per year is a lot money to show us a debt of over $4 trillion. It might be wise for the Chaplain to teach the Congress the Ten Commandants, starting with Number 8: "Thou shalt not bear false witness against thy neighbor." It appears as though they have never read them. Surely this would reduce some of the shouting and finger pointing.

The President should not allow the elected ones to go on TV or have articles printed in newspapers without first attending meetings by all concerned. The people need to hear results, not some so and so on TV trying to net some personal gain or bad mouth his opponent. The President should see to it that he and the Vice President (and all other officials in Washington) will be seen on TV or in the newspaper only to report results for the nation and people.

The President should be seen on TV every December 31st thanking the American people for their untiring effort and support rendered to Washington for the prior year. All we are hearing now is a plea for more tax dollars for the Washington establishment to waste.

We need a President who will restore the once thriving American industries that proudly displayed the Made in America label. We need farms and ranches, oil and gas production in full swing like they were before and during WWII. America needs good paying jobs again.

America needs to be selling government bonds and we need a President that will restore and promote this policy. Let the loan sharks howl all they want. Loan sharks are no match for government bonds. Government bond revenue was how WWII was fought and won. No way this country could have fought and won WWII without the bond program. The loan sharks in this country give us an umbrella on a sunny day and take it away when it rains. Let's put bonds back in the market in full swing so our government will stand on both legs again like it used to. The loan sharks have proven to all that they could care less. We need a President who knows how to organize, who will hang tough when the going gets rough, be able to take the bitter with the sweet, and who will always give 100% in all tasks.

The President should run our country like a business, with proper accounting of all monies, giving the people a report every six months on how much money was spent and how much money is left for future uses. The President should throw out the free loaders who are being paid the big bucks just to hang around without a sense of shame. This is a much needed policy.

The President needs to make some changes in Congress. Two congressmen per state and two clerks per senator is enough. Why pay 535 in the Congress when 100 is enough to do the job? This would greatly improve the efficiency in Congress and the people would not have to deal with the present back biting and their noise. This would also save the taxpayers over $2 billion per year. The states already have governors and city mayors on the payroll to be responsible for what is going on in their states and cities. There are too many on the payroll in Washington just to live high on the hog and make noise. The governors should be the number one advisor to the President anyway.

We need a President who will put a stop to the large number of immigrants (practically unchecked) allowed into this country. He can get this done by posting U.S. Military Forces along the Rio Grande until fences can be constructed to keep the illegal aliens out. The same thing could be done to our shores.

The President should appoint a Secretary of Defense that knows military operations and will not get himself involved in politics. The one from Wyoming turned his office over to the Joint Chiefs of Staff. He was seen on TV voicing the need for more cuts in the military. Because it was a presidential election year he made it sound like he could defend America with Wyoming horse droppings. It would be a great learning experience for the Secretary of Defense to spend two weeks per year in the field with troops, crawling on his belly, shooting for record on the rifle range, sleeping on the ground, with one canteen of water per day. Then, on the fourteenth day, make it known that he is ready for more of the same. All other secretaries should be made to do the same in their departments.

Finger pointing and shouting matches should be avoided in Congress. Instead, they should be encouraged to use their fists in disagreements. In 1859, a U.S. Senator from California was killed in a duel with a Judge. The Judge returned to his bench and the dead Senator got a ride to the cemetery. Yes, duels are needed in Washington, between the Republicans and the Democrats, to effect a more sincere manner of settling differences than what we are seeing now. Betting on the sidelines would make it even more interesting.

The President should institute a policy that would make all tax money payable at the end of the year. That would tear up the playhouse for the Congress to waste the taxpayer's money all year long.

Those that want to support their ancestors will have to pay the bill themselves. Our President needs to make sure this is the policy. It would be applicable to immigrants. The president also needs to make sure there is only one type of birth certificate for all Americans, and that it pertains to all skin colors. This would reduce much of the present howling and angling for free rides.

We need a plan for the future. Resettling people from congested cities out into the country when possible should be the goal. The big cities of America are full of problems and invitations to crime and divorce. The old song sings: "Good Gal, you continue to the city till you lose your happy home." That song should be played to the high steppers daily. Low rental housing should be built on the outskirts of towns and cities away from the other homes.

The President should also be preparing a plan that would allow only one person per family to be employed. America is now overpopulated with high unemployment. So many of the American jobs are now overseas and in Mexico. A plan needs to be prepared and placed on file for future use. Yes folks, those days are coming much sooner than we think.

We need a President who will protect all the natural resources left in our nation. In the 1950's the Republicans in the White House went into mass production in all areas, wasting our resources left and right. America is now dangerously short on some of these foolishly wasted resources because there was no plan for the future. Some American cities are unable to find land for use as waste dumps. The officials in Washington will do anything to get re-elected it seems. To hear the Republicans tell it, they are the conservatives. They sure didn't practice conservation in the 1950's during the mass productions.

We need a President that will make it known that the American working class and other taxpayers make Washington. A President that will deny that Washington makes the American people.

Future planning for the nation and people's needs is long overdue. There are hundreds of babies born in America every day. Industry needs to be restored to its WWII era heyday if we are to get away from the "rob Peter to pay Paul" syndrome. The current Good Ole Boys and Gals have failed us.

We also need a President that will change the voting in America to be on Saturdays. There is far too much money being wasted on reelections, conventions, and howling. The American flag takes a beating during a Presidential election year. Once, the campaign is over, the flag is rarely seen until the next election. Just take a look at how many flags are displayed on Memorial and Veterans Day and on 14 June. The numbers are shamefully small.

We need a President who will turn the welfare programs over to the state governors and require the program to be identical in all 50 states. This includes the same procedures for courts and fighting crime. Procedures for all crimes must be the same for all the nation if headway is to be made. The present city by city, county by county, etc., is not getting the job done. The current system is very costly and difficult to obtain results. Positive action in all of these areas is long overdue.

At present there are those that make a better living on the welfare system than those who go to work every day. The Governors and Mayors must be turning their heads. This is their responsibility, not Washington's. Parents must also be held responsible for everything their children do, or fail to do, regardless of time or place. There should be no more free rides for the irresponsible parents. Let's stop baiting for votes with welfare promises, or taking money for elections without knowing where the money is coming from.

It must also be decided what is "poor" in America. There are some people who play "poor" to keep from working for a living. For many it's simply a gravy train. Low rental housing is full of people that take advantage of the system. Couples divorce, get on handouts, and then live together. They even get the snow removed from their parking lots by a person on the civil service payroll. Some of the people living in the low rental housing projects are retired military, with a good sized retirement check each month. We need good people on the job here to insure things are on the up and up.

What is considered "poor" in America? Our current system is inviting people to be poor in this nation. This situation is growing out of control and can only be stopped by responsible parents. Let's keep Washington out of the Governors and City Mayor's business. The gravy train is getting longer every day. Make the welfare recipients show a job application (a recent one) before they can receive more handouts. This is one good way to get a handle on the current freeloading.

Lowering and raising taxes is like patching old trousers; eventually they will have to be thrown out. We need a President that is aware of this. Many states now are relying on lotteries. This doesn't work, either. Not all the players will win and the governors will end up feeding the losers anyway. The working class will have to pick up the tab. There isn't a better way for the governors to become trouserless. Male governors will do all right in their underwear, but the female governors might find it a bit airish. Listen up. There is no substitute for the American industries to keep the nation on sure footing. Those elected officials who approved of American businesses moving overseas and to Mexico will have to eat plenty of rice, beans, chili, tacos, and tortillas, three times a day, to meet the needs of America and keep her standing on both legs.

In closing, one of the past Presidents said, "America will never fall from without; if she falls, it will be from within." The current 537 presidents (elected officials) are busy doing just that. Mr. Past President, farsight wins. The only way to clean this big mess is for Americans to join one of the many coalitions available to them and vote the present officials out of office. New officials will have trouble making headway under the current system. The ones responsible for the problems in Washington are in charge of the Congress and Senate and continue to tell them what to do.

The people of Washington are the problem now. No more lawyers in Congress to represent us. This alone is 95% of our nation's problems. Giving our old system an overhaul would be a waste of time, and lost time cannot be recalled. It is time to tell our old failures goodbye.

FIRST LADIES

There appears to be plenty of ideas on what the First Lady of our nation should be. The First Lady should show warmth and love towards the people and be of help where possible. The First Lady showing off the family pet is not in good taste. We (the American public) have had to endure this situation a bit much of late. The current First Lady does not indulge in the practice of exploiting the family pet and should be commended for it.

First Ladies should be talking to families, especially the children, not talking political garbage. Instead of going overseas with the President, the First Lady should remain here where she can do more to help the needy.

It is not necessary for the First Lady to go abroad, assuming the President can sit through a meeting without falling out of his chair. Those who have traveled abroad made it appear that all American women live like the first ladies do. We all know this is not so.

One First Lady went on TV to ask the American public to stop using drugs. That alone proved the First Lady was unaware of the severity of the drug problem in America. Those who practice good know-how had to feel a little sorry for her. The drug problem in America will not be solved simply by the asking. Instead, it will take hard, positive actions to eliminate it.

Some of our first ladies did a good job because they talked of the benefits of good housekeeping and child rearing. We have all but forgotten those first ladies who failed to preach the merits of domestic accomplishments. There was once a First Lady who never cooked a meal or made her own bed. She was terribly out of place in Washington.

The First Lady should be the ideal Stateswoman and her husband, the President, should be the ideal Statesman for our nation. When we had a President who was a true Statesman, the people of our nation were on a much firmer footing. Today's party system splits the nation and is no good for America.

STATE GOVERNORS

Presently our state governors are not being properly utilized. They could be the first-hand-know-how to the President if all 50 of them were included in the planning of programs for our country. The Congressmen do not know enough of what needs to be done on a state by state basis. The governor is paid to know what is going on in his state. He also has the mayors and city managers to help him. By using the governors cooperation with the President a decline could be seen in the current waste of money. We have nothing to lose by trying.

If we used the knowledge of our governors more wisely, we could reduce the Congress to two Congressmen per state. That alone would save the taxpayers over $2 billion per year. This would increase the efficiency in Congress. There are far too many living high on the hog in Washington D.C. and it's time to put a stop to it.

The money now used to pay Congressmen could be put to a much better use elsewhere. Surely our Congressmen have counted all the manure piles, along with some other useless projects. From now on 100 Congressmen are enough. The other 435 Congressmen are like stumps in the orchard: unproductive, in the way, and worthless.

Abolishing the Internal Revenue Service would put the American people in control of their money like it used to be.

Printed in the USA
CPSIA information can be obtained
at www.ICGtesting.com
JSHW082353140824
68134JS00020B/2048

9 781681 623443